THE
SERVANT
KING

THE SERVANT KING

VERNE NESBITT

Whitaker House

THE SERVANT KING

Verne Nesbitt Ministries
3844 W. Michelle Drive
Glendale, AZ 85308

ISBN: 0-88368-436-5
Printed in the United States of America
Copyright © 1996 by Verne Nesbitt

Whitaker House
580 Pittsburgh Street
Springdale, PA 15144

Acknowledgments

Without the encouragement, inspiration, and counsel of my precious helpmeet, Diane, this book would never have seen the light of day. Her input to this work, to say nothing of to my life, has been invaluable.

My special thanks to Jay Cunningham and David Hanson, patron saints in the truest sense.

To all those faithful and loyal friends and loved ones who, through the years, have made it possible for me to devote myself to the study and ministry of God's Word, thank you, and may the Lord richly bless you.

And most of all, thank You, Lord Jesus, for using me as Your instrument to express this vision of Yourself.

Contents

*Life has value only when it has
something valuable as its object.*

—Hegel
Philosophy of History

Chapter 1

Finding Majesty
in Humility

"Take My yoke upon you and learn from Me,
for I am gentle and humble in heart,
and you will find rest for your souls."
—Matthew 11:29 (NIV)

*T*he humility of Christ" is a foreign phrase to many today, even in the church. To some, Christ's humility is equated with Christ's meekness, although in reality they are two different concepts. To others, speaking of the humility of Christ evokes thoughts of Jesus' most embarrassing moments, instances of perceived weakness in what is an otherwise admirable life. In the following verses, for example, His humiliation is often thought to be weakness:

9

³² *"He was led as a sheep to the slaughter;*
and as a lamb before its shearer is silent,
so He opened not His mouth.
³³ *"In His humiliation His justice was*
taken away, and who will declare His gen-
eration? For His life is taken from the
earth."   (Acts 8:32–33)

In contrast to this erroneous idea of Christ
being weak because He is humble, I would like
to focus on our Lord's humility from a different perspective, the one portrayed in Matthew
11:29: *"For I am gentle and humble in heart."*

According to *Merriam-Webster's Collegiate
Dictionary*, to experience humility is to have or
express "the quality or state of being humble,"
but that is not as helpful as it could be due to
the fact that there are several definitions for
the word *humble*. To be humble can imply
having a consciousness of one's own defects or
shortcomings. But another, lesser-used definition of being humble identifies the heart of the
word, especially where our Savior's humility is
concerned.

humble *adj.* lowly; low in condition, rank, or
position; reflecting or expressing a spirit of
deference or submission.

This is the definition that comes the closest to
describing our Lord as He is pictured for us in

God's Word. It is that definition with its implications and connotations I have tried to sum up in the title of this book, *The Servant King*.

But titles and definitions do little to minister to the heart and soul of the follower of Christ. It is Jesus alone—in His humility—who can do that, and that is precisely what He does. He ministers to the hearts and souls of His disciples simply by being who He is, the Humble One. When He walked on the face of the earth, Jesus did what He did because He was who He was, the Humble One.

Ministry that amounts to anything must flow from the heart. To state this in another way, God is more interested in who we are than in what we are doing. That is precisely what the Bible conveys to us about Jesus our Lord: everything He did came from who He was at heart. He didn't do things in order to become somebody. He became what He had not been before—low in position, lowly—in order that He might do what He did—save, heal, redeem, and deliver.

Since the time of my conversion at nineteen, I have been awestruck by the humility of our Lord. It's my educated guess that those who have been similarly overwhelmed by our Savior's lowliness are those who have the least trouble acknowledging His lordship over them.

After having observed thousands of believers firsthand, I am convinced it is the humbleness of our Lord that motivates the faithful to yield up their lives to Him—often literally—no matter how difficult the mission He has called them to.

I remember that as a schoolboy I was somewhat overwhelmed as well, but it wasn't who Jesus was that mystified me back in those days. At that time, my thoughts generally revolved around the mysteries of the universe: What is reality? Where did I come from? What makes things tick? How did everything come into being in the first place?

One of my most vivid memories of this sense of awe and wonder came from watching a movie in my preteens. That experience combined elements of the mysterious and unknown with my first thoughts about aspects of deity in a profound way. I don't remember exactly how old I was or the name of the movie, but I do remember I was fascinated by the opening scene. It took place high above the heavens. Several horsemen, who were supposed to be gods, sat bareback on trusty steeds, talking impassively with each other. As they peered through space and the atmosphere of the earth below, they conjectured about what might happen to various people if they were to intervene in the daily course of human affairs. Of course, the rest of the movie demonstrated the consequences of their decision and their subsequent meddling.

Even though I had a formal church upbringing, I remember speculating about the possibility of such a thing. Did one or more powerful beings determine the destiny of mankind? Did lofty and lordly entities really patrol the universe on snow-white stallions (that idea was so appealing to me because I had always had a special love for horses), casually making decisions that would affect me? Or, was my fate in my own hands?

That, of course, led to yet other questions: Was there really a triune God as my Christian heritage had taught? If so, what connection did God have with my life on a day to day basis? Did God really care about what I did or which path I chose to take? If so, would He or could He intervene, one way or the other?

Whatever my evolving concept of deity may have been back in those days, as the years went by, I came to one unshakable conclusion: Any god worthy of my adoration would have to be mighty and powerful *beyond* my imagination. As it turned out, my conclusion had a lot going for it. The God whom I now gladly serve is preeminent beyond description. Indeed, theologians use high-sounding terms such as omnipresent, omnipotent, and omniscient to try to put into words the attributes of God. However, in reality He is so far removed from human conception that He is actually *"past finding out"* (Romans 11:33).

Nevertheless, now in my more "mature years," that which truly defies my imagination is not so much the power and majesty of God, but the humility of the Word who was God, yet who became a man, Christ Jesus.

That, actually, is what this study is all about. It seeks to trace how it came to be that the One who once inhabited the Ivory Palaces became a helpless, defenseless baby, lying in a manger, and how the all-knowing, all-powerful Creator of the universe chose to become a by-word for the sake of those He created.

Of course, I am also writing this book with the hope and prayer that God will somehow use it to lead others into a further realization of how awesome is this One whom we serve, this Jesus, this Humble One.

As for me, I am persuaded this sense of wonder that still pervades my soul will never cease as long as I live. The feeling of awe that sparked my imagination as a child even now permeates my thinking. New questions to ponder have replaced the old: What will the new heavens and the new earth be like? What will

His appearance be when we finally see Him *"face to face"* (1 Corinthians 13:12)? What will His *"new name"* (Revelation 3:12) be, and exactly what will it signify?

Actually, I really don't think that sense of awe and wonder will ever end. Rather, I think what I am experiencing now is just the beginning of heavenly wonders—things that God has in store for His children that will create a sense of delightful awe and wondrous surprise throughout all eternity.

I have gone through many stages in life, I suppose. In reality, however, I have only gone from being a child full of wonder to an adult full of wonder. Indeed, my sense of awe and wonder has led me to pursue hobbies like astronomy and degrees in the fields of philosophy and theology—to search out both the wisdom of men and the Book of Books from cover to cover. Yet, in all my pondering, studying, reading, and wondering, nothing has ever quite affected me as much as this wonder of wonders—the humility of Christ, my Savior.

I have a hunch that's the way it will always be.

Eternity is a terrible thought.
I mean, where's it going to end?

—Tom Stoppard
Rosencrantz & Guildenstern Are Dead

Chapter 2

Eternity in His Heart

*E*ternity—what a concept, what a thought-provoking idea! Have you ever given much thought to the idea of eternity? Most of us have, probably. We certainly have incorporated sayings such as "From here to eternity," "Eternally yours," and "It would take an eternity" into our everyday expressions. Apparently, eternity is on our minds a lot.

Still, how many of us understand what we're saying? Have any of us been able to really grasp the meaning of eternity? Or, is it one of those concepts, like infinity, that we mortals will never be able to comprehend, at least in this lifetime?

I remember as a teenager the idea of infinity was one that strained my whole thinking process. It was even more bothersome to me than the concept of eternity, although I always felt like the two—unending space (infinity) and time without end (eternity)—were somehow related. But, to me, at least, infinity was the more mind-boggling of the two concepts.

It seems as if it were just yesterday when my best friend and I were at one of our favorite hangouts, Encanto Park in Phoenix, stretched out on a cool, grassy knoll. The sky on that warm, spring night was cloudless and growing darker by the moment. One by one, tiny points of light unceremoniously, but nevertheless mysteriously, emerged from the surrounding blackness. Even for teenage guys who mostly thought and talked about girls, it was stimulating stuff.

At times like this, Ray and I would engage in one of our favorite pastimes, "philosophizing." I don't think we called it philosophizing back in those days, but that's what it was. I remember that, after lying there for some time, lazily staring as this wonder silently unfolded before my eyes, I said something like, "Ray, do you think space has a boundary out there somewhere? I mean, if you could travel forever in one direction, do you think you would eventually come to the end, where stars were no more and you couldn't go any farther?" I rushed on before he could give me his answer: "And if there were an end, a wall or boundary of some kind, then what's on the other side of the boundary? I really want to know!"

Eternity must be something like that. What was there prior to eternity? Apparently, some would call that a nonsensical question, because either eternity is or it isn't. There can't be anything before eternity or after eternity. The very idea of eternity conveys the impression of having no beginning or ending points.

Most of us are aware that the Judeo-Christian position on such issues teaches that God is eternal; He is without beginning or end. (Do you remember asking yourself questions such as, Who created God? or, Where did God come from?) However, this is where the formula becomes really complicated for most of us. Not only are we talking here about endless space and perpetual time, now we're talking about some *One* who has lived forever, a *Being* who is without beginning or end! These are fairly heady matters, I must say.

The God of Meaning and Purpose

Before we explore this any further, let me interject something that I believe is very relevant to our discussion. If most of us can be content with the idea that space somehow goes on and on, and if we can accept the concept of endless time, then why is it too much for some of us to believe that an uncreated Creator has always existed?

Let's even take this a step further here. For the sake of argument, let's say there really is no God; let's say the evolutionists and atheists are right. Where would that leave us? Simply put, it would leave us with perpetual time and endless space without rhyme, reason, or purpose!

How is it that we humans, who demand reasons and explanations for everything—in other words, we who think of ourselves as possessing a great deal of rhyme, reason, and purpose—can be so easily hoodwinked into believing that such an unsupported theory as godless evolution has any credence whatsoever? How is it that we, who proudly think of ourselves as being so profound, came about (quite by accident, mind you) in such a meaningless universe?

Eternity Defined

Before we get too carried away with such issues, let's get back to where we were. You'll remember that we were exploring the notion of eternity and how it relates to the God of biblical revelation.

What is fascinating to me is that when we look at the many biblical references to eternity, almost without exception we find "eternity," "eternal," and "everlasting" were translated from some form of the Greek word *aion,* which means an age or an epoch. The concepts of time and eternity conveyed in the Scriptures are actually complementary. Eternity is, in fact, the designation of an endless period of time. When *eternity* is used in referring to the past, it denotes the dim, distant past. In referring to the future, it conveys the notion of an age that goes on and on. In the Bible *eternity* never means time*less*; rather, it means an age or an epoch that continues forever.

"But wait a minute," I can just hear someone saying, "doesn't the Bible tell us that the day is coming when *'there should be time no longer'* (Revelation 10:6 KJV)?"

I'm glad you asked that! It leads me to make the following observation: As we have been employing the term *eternity,* we have been conveying the notion of an endless epoch, one that continues on and on. We'll use the phrase "lasting time" to communicate this idea.

However, the original Greek word for *time* in Revelation 10:6 is quite different. It is the

Greek term *chronos*, from which the English word *chronology* is derived. *Chronos* is the biblical term used to express the formal, scientific sense of time. For the sake of clarity, we'll call this "measurable time." In Revelation 10:6, we are told it is chronological, measurable time that will be no more.

Still, even lasting time doesn't just go on and on, all by itself. Not at all! What the Bible clearly teaches is that lasting time, or eternity, is really an expression of the nature of God.

Stop a moment to contemplate what has just been said. Eternity is not something that exists outside of God. Instead, the Bible tells us that eternity belongs to God and is part of Him:

[27] *The eternal God is your refuge, and underneath are the everlasting arms.*
    (Deuteronomy 33:27)

[17] *Now to the King eternal, immortal, invisible, to God who alone is wise...*
    (1 Timothy 1:17)

Returning to the questions with which my youthful friends and I occupied ourselves, we find there couldn't have been anything before God, even eternity. Simply stated, just as time is because God is, eternity is because God is!

Living Eternally

Now, notice how all of this relates to what the Bible calls *"eternal life."* Remember, the Lord proclaimed, *"I am the resurrection and the life"* (John 11:25). Jesus, by virtue of His resurrection, is living a life that has no end. That is why we could well say that Jesus doesn't "mark time." No, eternity is explicitly because Jesus lives!

Are we really grasping this? The biblical concept of eternity is not something obscure after all. When we think of eternity, we are never asked to entertain some fuzzy notion of a timeless past or a future that goes on and on and on, just for the sake of doing so. Rather, when we think of eternity, we are coached by the Bible to think of the God of eternity.

Just as you can't have resurrection life apart from the One who is the Resurrection, so also you can't have eternal life—that is, you can't live that life tomorrow or a thousand years from tomorrow—apart from the Eternal One. As long as you are in Christ and He is in you, you will not only live life and live it abundantly (John 10:10), but you will also live that life as long as He does. And, dear one, in case you haven't understood so far what I have been trying to say, that means forever!

> [12] *He who has the Son has life; he who does not have the Son of God does not have life.* [13] *These things I have written to you who believe in the name of the Son of God, that you may know that you have eternal life.*
> (1 John 5:12–13)

I would be remiss if I did not take just a moment to address a vital issue for perhaps only a few of you who are reading this book. If you do not know for sure that you have eternal life, I invite you to meet Jesus Christ, who said, *"I am the way, the truth, and the life"* (John 14:6). As you read these pages, I hope and pray you will open your heart to receive a special revelation of the Savior who loves you so much that He died for you so that you might live eternally with Him.

> [16] *For God so loved the world that He gave His only begotten Son, that whoever believes in Him should not perish but have everlasting life.* (John 3:16)

If, when you have finished reading this book, or at any point along the way, you realize that you are in need of Christ's saving grace, just talk to Him, acknowledge your sinful state, and ask Him to become your Lord and Savior. He will do it. That's what He died for.

Time and space are fragments of the infinite for the use of finite creatures.

—Henri Frederic Amiel
Journal, 16 November 1864

Chapter 3

The God of Time and Space

You have no doubt heard the saying, "Time flies when you're having fun!" But, did you know that there may be more truth than fiction in that old chestnut? We found that out when Albert Einstein came upon the stage of human history. Remember, it was Einstein who introduced a similar concept that has become perhaps as well-known: "Time is relative."

Why is it that time is relative? Perhaps a better question would be, What exactly is time relative to? According to the good professor's theory, time is relative to the observer of time or, to be even more precise, to the motion of the one who is observing. In turn, Dr. Einstein informed us, this is dependent on the notion

that in all of the known universe there is only
one physical property that is not relative—only
one thing that remains consistently constant—
and that is the speed of light.

Keep in mind as we consider these issues
that without the aid of certain kinds of objects
in the physical world—let's say, watches or
clocks or the sun as it moves in the sky—time
(measurable, chronological time) could not be
measured at all. Chronological time is evident
precisely because it is measurable!

This reminds us, doesn't it, of what our
Lord and Creator proclaimed right from the
beginning:

> [14] *Let there be lights in the firmament of the
> heavens to divide the day from the night;
> and let them be for signs and seasons, and
> for days and years.* (Genesis 1:14)

The speed of light is constant, but chronological time is relative. Yet, when we consider
under what circumstances time is measured
and who it is that is measuring it, this notion
of the relativity of time really becomes in-
triguing.

We could possibly get into a lot of techni-
cal jargon about this theory. Instead, let's refer
to a well-known illustration that graphically
demonstrates it—the paradox about twins.

Physicists explain it this way: if one of a set of twins remains on the earth while the other travels in a spaceship for ten years at a rate of speed that approaches the speed of light, the latter would return to find the earthbound twin fourteen years older than himself! (For more details, refer to the meticulous notes you jotted down in your high school physics class.) Thus, time is not constant; as we can see from this paradox, it cannot in any sense be thought of as an absolute.

Now, as we consider these things from the perspective of the Bible, we could well ask, Who else but God is the Constant of the universe? On top of that, we could assert that it is none other than God who is the Observer of the universe, as well!

A Very Large Being

Phillip Yancey has long been one of my favorite authors. In *Disappointment with God*,[1] his concept of a Very Large Being as the Observer of the universe lends a perspective that really gets the imaginative juices flowing.

Let's picture Yancey's theoretical Very Large Being (VLB) as standing straddled with

---

[1] Phillip Yancey, *Disappointment with God* (Grand Rapids: Zondervan, 1988), 186.

one foot on the earth and the other foot on a distant star. (Remember, this is a Very Large Being!) If we were to use our closest star, Proxima Centauri, in this illustration, we would still be talking about something more than 23 trillion miles away. Nevertheless, because of his size and vantage point, our VLB can easily observe both Earth and Proxima Centauri at the same time. However, if our VLB were to stomp on Proxima Centauri and completely snuff it out of existence, we on Earth wouldn't know it until we became aware of the absence of that star's light some four years later!

We don't need to take too big a leap to arrive at the point: the inference is that our theoretical VLB is indeed the infinite God of the universe. Needless to say, God is aware of all things at all times, but, just as obviously, everything that we experience in the physical world is relative to Him.

Now, keeping in mind that light is distinguished by the fact that its rate of speed is the only known constant in the universe, we need to be aware of yet another reality: it is a commonly accepted truism in the scientific world that nothing else in the universe is capable of attaining the incredible speed of light (sorry, *Star Trek* fans). The reason is simply that the faster something goes as it approaches the speed of light—which, as you know, is the rather exhilarating speed of over 186,000 miles per second—the more its mass will increase. As a matter of fact, physicists assure us that if something ever could attain the velocity of light, there would be an instantaneous result: that thing would become extended infinitely, totally filling space.[2]

The Bible informs us that God is light (1 John 1:5). The Bible also makes it clear that God is infinite. Hmmmmmmm.

With all these things in mind, let's take a few more steps toward understanding how the infinite God can simultaneously be the God of both time and space.

The Space-Time Continuum

We saw in the first chapter that eternity is because God is. Now, as we continue to search His Word, we find what we might have expected. That is, the same thing holds true of the space-time continuum: it exists because God is—except with a really delightful slant!

To be sure, we of the Judeo-Christian faith assert that God our Creator is transcendent, or

---

[2] In theory, *if* a particle could travel faster than the speed of light, it would emit light, an effect dubbed by physicists as the "Cherenkov radiation."

that Almighty God is distinct from His creation. For example, we read the following:

> [2] *Before the mountains were brought forth,*
> *or ever You had formed the earth and the*
> *world, even from everlasting to everlasting,*
> *You are God.* (Psalm 90:2)

> [27] *But will God indeed dwell on the earth?*
> *Behold, heaven and the heaven of heavens*
> *cannot contain You!* (1 Kings 8:27)

Yet, the same Bible testifies that God is also omnipresent in His universe. Simply stated, this means that God is everywhere at once. For example, we find this expression of the Lord:

> [24] *"Can anyone hide himself in secret*
> *places, so I shall not see him?" says the*
> *LORD; "Do I not fill heaven and earth?"*
> *says the LORD.* (Jeremiah 23:24)

What are we to make of this? Does the Bible contradict itself by maintaining that God is omnipresent in the space-time continuum, yet transcends His creation? Hardly! As a matter of fact, if you look closely, you'll see the glory of what is declared.

> [15] *For thus says the High and Lofty One*
> *who inhabits eternity, whose name is Holy:*

The God of Time and Space

*"I dwell in the high and holy place, with
him who has a contrite and humble spirit."*
(Isaiah 57:15)

How our Lord must enjoy His creation!
Even as we see how eternity serves God as His
habitation, we find that space is the robe with
which He clothes Himself; the Bible proclaims
He wears the light of the universe as His garment (Psalm 104:2). Just think of it, at some
point in ages past, our Lord no doubt reflected
on what it would be like to clothe Himself with
the Milky Way and make the Pleiades His
starry crown!

With this thought in mind, please take the
time to meditate upon the following:

21 *Have you not known? Have you not
heard? Has it not been told you from the
beginning? Have you not understood from
the foundations of the earth?*
22 *It is He who sits above the circle of the
earth...who stretches out the heavens like a
curtain, and spreads them out like a tent to
dwell in.* (Isaiah 40:21–22)

The Emperor's New Clothes

I have always had a keen interest in astronomy. One evening several years ago, I began browsing through an oversized volume my

oldest daughter had given me as a gift. I was particularly delighted with this book because it was full of beautifully-colored photographs of distant celestial wonders. On this particular night, as I was carefully reading the text that accompanied the stunning pictures, I was struck with the fact that no human eye had ever directly observed these breathtaking phenomena! I was startled when I learned that these glorious images could only be seen because sophisticated cameras tracked, sometimes for days at a time, the light these celestial objects emitted—light that was far too distant and far too faint to be observed with the unaided eye.

I remember that, after pondering the meaning of my discovery, some nights later I prayed aloud to the Lord, all the while gazing at a brilliantly star-studded sky. "Dear Lord," I said, recalling what I had just recently learned, "I really don't understand something. There is all of this vast beauty in space, and yet not one person has ever actually seen it. Why is it there in the first place?"

Now, I don't know what you think about the Lord answering back on occasions like this, but it's my firm conviction He said to my inner man something like, "My son, I enjoy it all very much, thank you!"

Yet, even though the Lord must take great satisfaction in His creation, the day is coming when it, too, will come to an end, because even the heavens and the highest heavens have become polluted with the presence of His Enemy. Have you ever been anxious to shed your beautiful clothes because foul-smelling odors had invaded and soiled the very garments you wore? Likewise, when the Lord returns on that great day—because Satan has defiled God's heaven—He has promised that He will make all things new, even His robes!

> [10] *You, LORD, in the beginning laid the foundation of the earth, and the heavens are the work of Your hands.*
> [11] *They will perish, but You remain; and they will all grow old like a garment;*
> [12] *Like a cloak You will fold them up, and they will be changed. But You are the same, and Your years will not fail.*
>
> (Hebrews 1:10–12)

Even though we may be awed by the wonder of God's creation, apparently it will be nothing compared to the *"new heavens and a new earth in which righteousness dwells"* (2 Peter 3:13).

I wonder what our Lord's new garments will look like?

*Action springs not from thought,
but from a readiness for responsibility.*

—Dietrich Bonhoeffer
Letters and Papers from Prison

Chapter 4

"In the Beginning Was the Word"

In the beginning was the Word, and the Word was with God, and the Word was God.
— John 1:1

W hy do you suppose so much has been preached, written, and taught on just this one little verse of Scripture, penned so many centuries ago by *"the disciple whom Jesus loved"* (John 21:20)?

At least part of the answer must lie deep within the heart of the child of God. Most Christians seem to share the ongoing conviction that much is at stake in having a proper understanding of this particular verse. Indeed, this profound portion of Holy Writ has been responsible for unraveling at least some of the mysteries of the Godhead for generation after generation of earnest inquirers.

Of course, the apostle John knew when he began his account that others had written about the Lord, but the Spirit of God had made it clear that it was John's turn to take pen in hand. He knew beyond the shadow of a doubt that he had something crucial to add to the church's understanding of who Jesus is.

Even so, I doubt that John was feeling particularly eloquent the day he began his tribute. I even doubt that he had a desire to become philosophical. Granted, he was excited and motivated. Most of all, however, John was inspired, but where was he to begin? How could he convey to others what he knew so well? What exactly would he share about this One who had so utterly changed his life? What could he say that would make others come to realize just how awesome his Lord's sacrifice was? Then, mightily moved by the Spirit of Truth, John discerned the whisper in his heart to begin at the beginning! *"In the beginning..."*

It doesn't take a scholar to realize that in writing as he did, John was alluding to the first book of the Bible. You see, he had determined it was best to tell us about the Savior from the perspective of eternity past. What better place to start than the Book of Beginnings, Genesis? Carefully touching his pen to the ink, he immediately proceeded with this fascinating disclosure: *"In the beginning was the Word, and the Word was with God, and the Word was God."*

Now, there is no question here about two points. First, due to a later verse in this introduction to his gospel, we know John was writing specifically about Jesus:

[14] *And the Word became flesh and dwelt among us, and we beheld His glory, the glory as of the only begotten of the Father, full of grace and truth.* (John 1:14)

John's second point was that this Jesus, before He became Jesus, existed as God. In so saying, John informed us about something we may otherwise have missed: Jesus wasn't always known as "Jesus" or "the Christ." In the beginning, John apprised us, Jesus was *"the Word."* If we had been privileged to be there in the beginning, we would have had a difficult time identifying *"the Word"* with the infant who would one day be born in a stable or with the man whom Jesus grew to be. In fact, John said that the Word is none other than the One who created man and brought the universe into existence in the first place. (See John 1:3.)

John was saying that the One everyone now calls Jesus had actually existed in eternity past—not as a man born of woman, but as Almighty God! The apostle addressed this very theme repeatedly in his gospel. Yes, as the other gospel writers had testified, Jesus was born of a virgin (Isaiah 7:14; Matthew 1:23). Yes, He was God's *"only begotten Son"* (John 3:16). Yes, He was God in the flesh (1 Timothy 3:16; 1 John 4:2). But, before He became the Son of Man, Jesus was, as the Holy Spirit testifies through yet another writer, *"in the form of God"* (Philippians 2:6).

I AM WHO I AM

Indeed, Jesus was none other than Yahweh! (*Yahweh* is now generally accepted as the most probable transliteration and pronunciation of the divine tetragrammaton, YHWH, God's personal name. Many, however, still prefer the more familiar *Jehovah*.) The important thing to grasp here is that God's personal name is actually a Hebrew verb that signifies "I AM," or the derivation, "I AM WHO I AM."

Notice how John was careful to record the words of our Lord on a rather telling occasion: *"Most assuredly, I say to you, before Abraham was, I AM"* (John 8:58). Many have assumed that, in so saying, Jesus was merely making it clear that He existed before Abraham was born. From the perspective of those who wanted to stone Him to death for blasphemy, that claim would have been quite enough—of that you can be sure. However, what Jesus was actually saying was: "I not only existed before Abraham, but I was also the One who appeared to Abraham as Yahweh, the great I AM."

Observe, for example, how Jesus' words deliberately correspond with the revelation Moses received from Yahweh about His name:

> ¹³ *Then Moses said to God, "Indeed, when I come to the children of Israel and say to them, 'The God of your fathers has sent me to you,' and they say to me, 'What is His name?' what shall I say to them?"* ¹⁴ *And God said to Moses, "I AM WHO I AM." And He said, "Thus you shall say to the children of Israel, 'I AM has sent me to you.'"* (Exodus 3:13–14)

This truth becomes even more apparent when we read the Record concerning the night of Jesus' betrayal. Tough professionals had come to seize Jesus by force. Trained to control the most violent criminals effectively, they came upon Jesus and His disciples who were meekly praying in a hillside olive grove. But, read the unexpected events that happened:

⁴ *Jesus therefore, knowing all things that would come upon Him, went forward and said to them, "Whom are you seeking?"*
⁵ *They answered Him, "Jesus of Nazareth." Jesus said to them, "I am He"...*
⁶ *Now when He said to them, "I am He," they drew back and fell to the ground.*

(John 18:4–6)

Doesn't the reaction of these Jewish soldiers, who were the chief priests' trained elite, strike you as being rather inconsistent with the expected response, *"I am* He"? But one has only to look at a more literal translation of this same verse (as any non-Greek reader can do by simply consulting a standard Greek/English interlinear text), or note that in most versions the word "He" is typeset differently from the rest of the text (indicating that it was not in the original manuscripts), to make some sense of the reaction of these disciplined troops: *"Now when He said to them, 'I AM,' they drew back and fell to the ground."*

Only one explanation makes sense for the completely unexpected and dramatic response of those who had come to hunt Jesus down. This crack unit of the Temple Guard had met their match. Actually, their worst nightmares had just come true! They found themselves opposing none other than *"the radiance of God's*

glory and the exact representation of his being"
(Hebrews 1:3 NIV). What might have been your
reaction if you had been one of those soldiers?

Eternity Past

In light of this disclosure by God's precious Holy Spirit, let me ask you this: What
have you imagined when you have heard Jesus
described as "the second person of the Trinity"? Have you seen Him in your mind's eye in
eternity past, prior to His appearance on
Earth, as a thirty-three-year-old man—or, for
that matter, as any kind of man? Or, have you
perhaps even pictured Him existing as an infant, waiting for just the right time to be born
of the Virgin?

If we have imagined Him in eternity past
as resembling a human being in any fashion,
we have yet to allow our imaginations to become subject to God's sacred revelation. Indeed, it was our Lord Himself who clarified the
issue of whether or not God may be anthropo-
morphized (attributed with human characteristics) by asserting, *"God is Spirit"* (John 4:24).

We must not envision our precious Savior
as having existed as a heavenly Man, complete
with bodily parts, or even a so-called "spirit-
man," waiting to be born. Rather, it was none

other than Yahweh, the great I AM, who stood ready to empty Himself for the sake of our redemption.

What I am proposing here for our continued contemplation is that the sacrifice of our Lord was far greater than we may have yet imagined. Indeed, according to the Scriptures —as well as the testimony of the saints down through the ages—the humiliation of our Lord in emptying Himself is that which has startled the angels, muddled the Enemy, and caused grown men to weep as they realized just how much they had taken the Lord's coming to Earth for granted.

*A journey of a thousand miles
begins with a single step.*

—Chinese Proverb

Chapter 5

The Emptying

*Have this attitude in yourselves which was also
in Christ Jesus, who, although He existed in
the form of God, did not regard equality with
God a thing to be grasped, but emptied Himself,
taking the form of a bond-servant,
and being made in the likeness of men.*
—Philippians 2:5–7 (NAS)

The sweet psalmist of old exalted his Creator when he sang, *"By the **word** of the LORD the heavens were made, and all the host of them by the breath of His mouth"* (Psalm 33:6).

One contemporary Bible scholar, commenting on Genesis 1:3, made this observation: "The Word Himself is the verb in the statement, *'and God **said**.'"* If we carefully compare the first, third, and fourteenth verses of the first chapter of John's gospel, something else becomes clear: *"The Word became flesh"* (v. 14) is a carefully stated proclamation that declares *"the Word,"* the Creator of all flesh (vv. 1, 3), fully participated in that which He created to a degree beyond natural man's comprehension.

Yet, this is a picture even Christians are not quite prepared for because it contains a perspective, a dimension, that speaks of majesty and mystery all rolled into one. It stirs a part of our beings too seldom touched. If we turn it just so, this picture catches the light of God's Spirit in such a way that it reflects a holy beam straight into the recesses of the inner man. When seen from this perspective, it truly takes our breath away as the incalculable cost of our redemption suddenly dawns on us!

In light of this glorious vision, it is hard to imagine why so much theological debate has been generated over Philippians 2:5–7, the passage quoted at the beginning of this chapter. Yet, even I got caught up for a while in debating the pros and cons of what has come to be known as "kenosis theology," which is so-called because the phrase *"emptied Himself"* (v. 7 NAS; RSV) is translated from the Greek word *kenosis.* How sad it is when we become consumed, in an emotionally detached way, with the theology of God rather than the God of theology!

What this majestic passage of Scripture in Philippians speaks of would be unutterable if it were not for the Holy Spirit's voice. Still, many have become preoccupied with the meaning of the term *kenosis* as it pertains to Jesus. Some insist He did indeed empty Himself of being in the form of God, while others steadfastly maintain that such a notion is impossible. They reason that if Christ had truly *"emptied Himself"* of His divinity, or even the prerogatives (the exclusive powers and privileges) of Deity, He would have ceased to be God. They insist that Christ *"emptied Himself"* by taking on something that He did not have before. Ironically, these theologians would tell us that addition, not subtraction, is the key to *kenosis*.

I propose that the only commentary we really need on this stirring passage in Philippians is the one the Bible itself provides. Another revealing verse simply says this:

> [9] *For you know the grace of our Lord Jesus Christ, that though He was rich, yet for your sakes He became poor, that you through His poverty might become rich.*
> (2 Corinthians 8:9)

Such a simple statement, yet so profound!

The Poverty of Christ

"Let there be light" (Genesis 1:3) came the thunderous decree! He who was the Word in Action, the Eternal Verb, thus spoke into existence the first of His created works. Yet, in Bethlehem several millennia later, no fiats were majestically pronounced. Only the cries of a newborn could be heard wafting into the night air. In His infant birth the eternal Word humbled Himself to become what He had never been before, but what He must forever remain, *"the Son of Man"* (John 1:51).

Little is to be gained from speculating whether an infant lying in a cow stall could have exercised the exclusive powers and privileges of Deity. To ask such a question indicates we have missed what these Scriptures are all about. Humility is the absence of self-assertion. Poverty is the antithesis of wealth. It is the Bible itself that stuns us with the revelation that our Lord, of His own volition, became poverty-stricken from the very instant of His conception!

Why is it we humans make an attempt to be erudite about things we're never going to be able to comprehend until we are in heaven anyway? Even worse, in our attempt to be so learned, we are probably neglecting the very thing we are supposed to be learning in the first place! Why can't we exercise the mind of Christ, as we are exhorted to do, by putting others before ourselves? Many of us would rather argue, debate, and get caught up in a spirit of religiosity than meditate upon the astonishing reality that *"though He was rich, yet...He became poor"* (2 Corinthians 8:9).

So much more is going on here than a mere battle of ideologies. If we fail to grasp the essence of what this passage is all about, then it won't make any difference if someone wins or loses a theological debate. What is at stake here is whether or not we can appreciate this one fact: Christ's poverty provides the wherewithal for our precious provision.

Issues of the Heart

It was that great Christian philosopher and scientist Blaise Pascal who observed, "The heart has its reasons which reason does not know." When I first became a believer and began to meditate upon the magnificent sacrifice my Lord had made for me on the cross of Calvary, I found myself vacillating between two irreconcilable conclusions—one that apparently originated in my heart of hearts and the other in my head.

My religious heritage and formal orthodox training had left me with an intellectual account that was contradictory to my emotions about the cross, which took the edge off of my excitement and joy. I tried to imagine heaven as it must have been before Jesus came to Earth. I could visualize the Father and the Son to some degree with my mind's eye. And somewhere, somehow, of course, was the Holy Spirit, although I must confess that He was the most difficult part to imagine. There they were, the Trinity. Together, the Father, the Son, and the Holy Spirit looked across the expanse of time at the sorry mess humanity would get itself into and determined to do something about it. (Does that sound vaguely familiar?) So, the Son volunteered to come to Earth by way of the Virgin Birth. Once here, He bore our sins on the cross and died, only to rise again and return triumphantly to heaven.

In my mental scenario, everything remained in or returned to its prior state. Yes, Christ's sacrifice on the cross was still a fundamental part of the story. However, as I pondered over its meaning, I felt compelled to conclude that it couldn't have been that big a deal for the second person of the Trinity. Certainly Jesus had suffered for a season, but He knew all the while He would return to His former state and things would go on pretty much the way they had before. The eternity of the future, I assumed, would probably be pretty much the same as eternity past. I was, of course, grateful for my salvation. As far as the Trinity was concerned, however, I surmised that nothing had been terribly affected by the fact that Jesus had come to Earth. So said my head.

On the other hand, however, my heart was awestruck with the realization that Jesus had died for me. His sacrifice became so real to me, His sufferings so terrible. He had shed genuine blood and died an actual death. It spoke to me of God's unremitting and unconditional love. It moved me to tears of repentance that became mingled with joyous tears of thanksgiving! Here it was, spelled out in black and white: He who knew no sin had become sin in order that I might become the very righteousness of God (2 Corinthians 5:21)! Even more, my heart somehow grasped that since Jesus ascended into heaven in bodily form and would return in the same way (Acts 1:11), He wasn't going to revert to His former state. As my heart realized that He had chosen to give all that up for me, I could do nothing except simply rejoice.

I'm so grateful that I listened to the truth in my heart!

*People only see what they
are prepared to see.*

—Ralph Waldo Emerson
Journals, 1863

*When we know exactly all a man's views
and how he comes to speak and act...
we lose respect for him,
though we may love him and admire him.*

—James Boswell
London Journal, 3 February 1763

Chapter 6

Bethlehem Made the Difference

Ask the angels. Ask Michael or Gabriel. See what they have to say. At least the heavenly host knows the difference our Lord's coming to Earth made in the heavenlies. They know things will never again be the same! They may not grasp it all, but they are keenly aware that Bethlehem did make a difference because they have seen it with their own eyes. They realize, for example, that our Savior's sacrifice did not begin at Calvary, or even in the Garden of Gethsemane. They know that when God became man at Bethlehem, at least two things took place that neither God nor man could ever alter or reverse.

To start, for the first time in all of time and eternity, God became a daddy. That is, God Almighty became the literal Father of a flesh-and-blood Offspring. (We will be dealing with this subject in far greater detail in the next chapter.)

Second, the Word who became flesh came to be what He had never been before—a man; a man born of a woman; a man born under the law; a man who died just as all other men die; yet, as no other man before or since, a man who was raised from the dead never to die again. (See 1 Corinthians 15:21.) Even more astounding is the fact that, from that time on, He would always remain a man.

Yes, our Lord reigns in heaven now, seated at the right hand of the Father. Yes, He is God the Son. But, just as surely, He is now and forevermore will be the Son of Man.

While the Scriptures make it clear our Lord was not born a son of Adam, nevertheless, Jesus was the bona fide son of Mary. On that wondrous night in Bethlehem of Judea, a brand-new relationship came into being. No doubt this was a relationship to which the Godhead had given much thought and creativity in eternity past. According to plan, a moment in the space-time continuum would occur when a mortal daughter of men would have formed within her body a son who, contrary to all human reasoning, would have neither a beginning nor an end.

Bethlehem Made the Difference

The Ultimate Contradiction

> [5] *Have this attitude in yourselves which was also in Christ Jesus,*
> [6] *who, although He existed in the form of God, did not regard equality with God a thing to be grasped,*
> [7] *but emptied Himself, taking the form of a bond-servant, and being made in the likeness of men.* (Philippians 2:5–7 NAS)

Thus, Jesus Christ, in His own person, is the ultimate contradiction. God the Word *"became flesh and dwelt among us"* (John 1:14)—the ultimate contradiction! He who had been in the form of God *"emptied Himself"*—the ultimate contradiction! The Master of the universe took upon Himself the form of a slave—the ultimate contradiction! He who was God became a bond servant to His Father—the ultimate contradiction!

In this incredible letter to the Philippians, when the apostle Paul referred to our Lord as He was in His preincarnate state (the state of our Lord before He became flesh), he did not write of One who was merely with God, but One who was *"in the form of God."* Then, in a deliberate and calculated fashion, the apostle set this fact in contrast to Jesus' current state, *"being...in the likeness of men."* Jesus Christ our Lord is now—dare we articulate it?—in the form of a slave! Just what was it our Lord refused to cling to? What was it that He chose to let go of? The text is clear: *"being in the form of God"* (v. 6 NKJV). In other words, one form of existence has forevermore replaced the other!

What can it all mean? Simply this: the sacrifice of Christ is unparalleled. Yes, let it be said again—the sacrifice of Christ is matchless, unequaled, unparalleled!

Having the Mind of Christ

The humility of Christ in the giving up of Himself goes far beyond the puny imagination of man. Yes, we have earnestly sought to find illustrations that demonstrate the magnitude of our Lord's sacrifice: for example, a human father who asks his only son to become an insect and remain an insect forever, for the sake of a lost and dying insect world. Still, not one of us has ever experienced anything remotely like Christ's sacrifice, so how could we expect to comprehend it? Indeed, the most eloquent poets become speechless as they attempt to express the sublimity of it all. Nevertheless, our Lord, who knows us better than we know ourselves, helps us even in these kinds of weaknesses (Romans 8:26)! Praise the Lord that His

Spirit teaches us, interpreting spiritual truths (1 Corinthians 2:13) to those yielded to Him.

> [9] *But as it is written: "Eye has not seen, nor ear heard, nor have entered into the heart of man the things which God has prepared for those who love Him."*
> [10] *But God has revealed them to us through His Spirit. For the Spirit searches all things, yes, the deep things of God.*
>   (1 Corinthians 2:9–10)

As we earnestly seek Him, prayerfully yielding ourselves to His Spirit's teaching, we can experience *"the mind of Christ"* (1 Corinthians 2:16)! That is exactly what the Lord promises His own—especially to us who are so needy and destitute in ourselves!

As we begin to see the picture and get a glimpse of what the Spirit of Truth has to say about the humility of our Lord, we may actually be moved to silence. We who may be tempted to be self-confident and erudite—and who would normally pride ourselves in having all the answers—may actually choose to still our thoughts and close our mouths. We may be so awed by this glorious and spell-binding revelation of God that we choose to take time to humbly reflect upon this awesome truth in a silence that becomes golden with a glorious, holy glow. No longer will we desire to get into theological debates; no more will we take sides. Instead, we will just kneel down worshipfully to absorb the wonder of it all.

But what am I?
An infant crying in the night;
An infant crying for the light,
And with no language but a cry.

—Alfred, Lord Tennyson
"In Memoriam A.H.H."

Chapter 7

"A Time to Be Born"

To everything there is a season,
A time for every purpose under heaven:
A time to be born, and a time to die.
—Ecclesiastes 3:1–2

I don't know whether it has ever struck you quite this way, but there is something wondrously odd about the order of our universe. While animals may have no problem bearing their young, our omnipotent God—in the beginning, at least—was quite incapable of doing the same.

Now, before you brand me as a heretic, allow me to explain what I mean. I hope to make it clear why God could never have started out by simply giving birth to His offspring. Just ask yourself, Can gods be born of God? Our dogs and cats readily give birth to their own kind, just as we humans give birth to ours. However, if there were something God could never do according to the pattern He had established, it would be to give birth to His own kind, and here is why. The Bible tells us that the very nature of God is to be without beginning or end. If God gave birth to another god-being, something new would necessarily come into existence that had never been before. That something would therefore have had a beginning. Thus, that being would not have been of God's own kind, with His identical nature, simply because it had a beginning.

Yes, God never had a beginning, and neither did the Word, who was with God and was God (John 1:1). God the Word did not suddenly spring into existence at some point in eternity past, due to the fact that He always existed. But, do not confuse the eternality of the Word with the reality that at a specific moment in chronological time *the Word became flesh* (John 1:14) when He *emptied Himself, taking the form of a bond-servant, and being made in the likeness of men* (Philippians 2:7 NAS).

Enter Adam

Surely you must have wondered, as I have on many occasions, why the Lord didn't just start out populating His universe with sons and daughters exactly like Jesus. Wouldn't it have been far simpler and less painful for all concerned to bypass Adam and Eve altogether? As gloriously fashioned as they may have been, they were, after all, merely creatures. (There is a vast difference between my wife making gingerbread men and her giving birth to our children!) Why didn't God just skip the Fall and all that rotten business and simply start out in a pristine state that would never end?

That would have been quite impossible as God had designed the scheme of things. As a matter of fact, it was absolutely necessary for Him to begin with Adam. It had been planned for perhaps countless eons that before God could bring His only begotten Son into the world, He had to create man.

The Plan of the Ages

The more you think about this, though, the more exciting it gets! When God created Adam, it was not the culmination of His works, but just the beginning. It was not according to God's plan for Him to give birth to sons; however, He could create Adam. Carefully fashioned, the first man became the prototype of the One who was to come.

Furthermore, Adam was made in God's image. This amazing creation, man, was able to exercise his will in total freedom! Just like his Creator, Adam was completely free to choose whom he would love.

Yet, the irony of it all is that unlike God (but very much like other creatures God made), Adam and Eve were able to bear offspring. Their offspring would, in turn, give birth to their own children and so on and so on, until that long-awaited and anticipated day when Mary would come upon the scene of history.

The Birth of Jesus

Have you ever given much thought to the fact that Jesus' entrance into the world was the same as all those who have been born before Him or since? Solely dependent upon His mother's ability to sustain Him in the womb, our Lord was literally tied to Mary with a cord of nourishment, and He was brought forth from her womb as all others are brought forth. Yes, Jesus clung to His mother's breast to suck the milk of life just as you or I may have. He was solely dependent upon others to bathe, clothe, and feed Him. In fact, at the first and at the last, He could barely move. At His birth His movement was restricted by swaddling clothes;

at His death His movement was restricted by
the spikes that nailed Him to the cross. He,
too, was limited to being in one place at a time.
Jesus was even carried off into a foreign land
by a fearful stepfather in order to escape the
lunacy of a pretender to the throne. He, too,
knew hunger and pain. And Jesus would come
to know, in one degree or another, what each
of us experiences in life, including and especially the temptation to be His "own man."

However, unlike all who came before Him
or all who would come after Him, Jesus came
with the most divine of purposes:

> [28] *The Son of Man did not come to be
> served, but to serve, and to give His life a
> ransom for many.* (Matthew 20:28)

To insure that we don't miss the point, let
me state it once again: the Word, God the Son,
who had no eternal beginning, nevertheless
had an earthly beginning as a helpless newborn. God finally brought forth His firstborn
Son through the vessel of His creation, Mary.

Oh, the wisdom of God! It is obvious that
without the Creator there would have been no
creation. Hopefully, however, it is becoming
clear to you that if God had not started out by
creating Adam, Jesus would never have been
born. First Adam, then Mary, then Jesus—it

67

had to be in that precise order according to the plan that had been established by God *"from the foundation of the world"* (Revelation 13:8).

The Father Heart of God

We need to consider another exciting element in all of this fantastic formula. The Bible makes it clear that God has always desired to be not merely a creator, but a father. As a matter of fact, the Scriptures declare that every family finds its motivation for existence as a family unit in the core of God's being. As it turns out, the holy, omnipotent God of the universe has "a daddy's heart."

What can be compared to having kids of one's own? (I'm talking about the human kind, of course.) What can be equated with the feeling of an ecstatic dad as he almost literally bursts with pride when his son or daughter first utters those two tiny syllables, "Da-Da"? You would think the little tyke had just recited the Gettysburg Address!

To be a father is not only one of life's greatest privileges, but it is also one of life's supreme purposes. And all of this springs from God's own purposeful heart. If we find great delight in our children, how much more must God take delight in having sons and daughters of His own. Is it too difficult to understand that God desires to have children who love Him in return, just as any of us would?

Of course, the Creator could have made Adam in such a way that the first man would have always loved Him. As a matter of fact, He could have created Adam so that Adam would never sin. It certainly would have been God's prerogative to do so. When you stop to think about it, He did create such sinless beings; they are called horses and chickens and ducks and cows. These creatures cannot sin against Him, but neither can they love Him, because love is not love unless it is freely given.

You could have been created to love and obey God always and unfailingly, but what satisfaction or joy could God possibly get from such an arrangement? If my wife were a robotic mate, I would be able to program her not only to love me, but—with a few simple adjustments—to guarantee that she would always be faithful. However, that's not what would thrill my soul and leave me in a constant state of matrimonial bliss. The bewildering delight is that my precious Diane chooses to love me. She doesn't have to; she wants to.

How much more our heavenly Father longs to have children who will love Him, not because they have to, but because they want to! He could have created us so that we would have no choice but to love Him. I suppose He could even now force our love, but such "love" would come forth from our souls stillborn.

The Father's Children

When you called out to the Lord Jesus Christ to save you, was someone pointing a gun at your head? When you asked Him to be the Lord of your life, was someone twisting your arm? If so, you can be sure God never intended it to be that way. God freely gave up His Son for your sake in order that you might just as freely receive His offer of eternal life. A gift is not truly a gift unless it is both freely given and freely received. God has never wanted to force you to be His child.

Nevertheless, God freely loved us, giving up His Firstborn in order that the terrible cost of our sins against Him might be dealt with justly. Now, because Christ has paid the price, our heavenly Father is free to express His love for us unreservedly for all of eternity without the barrier of sin separating us from being able to receive His lavish love.

Let's look at this from our human perspective. The moment I freely receive His precious Gift, not only is my spirit regenerated, but the very Spirit of God's only begotten Son is infused into my being, too! This incredible miracle happens when someone is truly *"born again"* (John 3:3, 7).

> [12] *To all who freely receive Jesus—who put their trust and confidence in His saving name—to such are given the ability or power to become God's children.*
> (John 1:12, author's paraphrase)

Consequently, ever since the cross and the empty tomb, the heavens are being peopled with God's offspring! There have always been angels, it seems, but now there are genuine, bona fide children roaming around the heavenlies. These are God's grateful kids who will love Him and praise Him throughout the endless ages, not because they have to or because they have no other choice, but because it is the fervent desire of their blood-bought hearts! Forever grateful for their redemption in Christ Jesus, these sons and daughters have freely chosen to live in unceasing praise and loving adoration of their heavenly Father.

The High Cost of Having Children

First Adam, then Mary, then Jesus, and now us—that precise order was essential. God couldn't have children—at least not at the start. But God could and did create Adam, with the full knowledge that not only would the first man turn against Him, but also that Adam's daughter Mary would one day humbly accept the privilege and responsibility of bearing the Savior. Jesus came, born of a woman, to woo us and win us, to save us and redeem us. But, even more than that, He came to transform us from the state of being mere creatures into the state of being true sons and daughters of God. What grace upon grace!

Obviously, if there had never been a Creator, there would have been no creation; but the fact is that Adam was made from the dust of the earth. If there had been no creation of offspring-bearing creatures, there would have been no such thing as sons and daughters; but the fact is that Mary was born a daughter of Adam's seed. If there had been no such thing as sons and daughters, the Son of Man could not have been born; but the fact is that Jesus was born of Mary. If there had been no Savior, there could never have been creatures who could be *"born again"*; but the fact is that the Spirit of Christ abides in us, by whom we are empowered to become God's very own offspring (John 1:12). The cycle of life is now complete because of Christ Jesus.

In our new birth, Jesus becomes at once our Savior and Friend, our Lord and King, and our Elder Brother!

Our Brother, the King

Our Brother, the King. You've met Him before, but perhaps you don't remember. Come, let me reacquaint you with Him. He is the One who became poor in order that you might become rich. He is the One who became like you in order that you could become like Him. He is the One who became the Son of Man in order that you might become a child of God. See Him over there, surrounded by His many siblings. You will be sure to recognize Him because He looks a lot like you—or, rather, you take after Him. At least, the family resemblance will be quite evident by the time you really do see Him face to face.

Remember, He is the One who came and gathered you up from the dust heap of your own making and breathed into you the breath of resurrection life. Do you see His nail-scarred hands, the deep wound in His side? You can't miss Him. Look, here He comes even now. He's coming to greet you as if you were a long-lost brother!

But, what's this? He has a towel in His hand, and He wants to wash your feet.

We need the faith to go a path untrod,
The power to be alone and vote with God.

—Edwin Markham
The Need of the Hour

Chapter 8

Our Trailblazer

*Looking to Jesus the pioneer and perfecter
of our faith...*
—Hebrews 12:2 (RSV)

For almost three hundred years America's trailblazers tracked through thousands of miles of wilderness, deserts, mountains, rivers, and forests in order to settle our nation. These pioneering frontiersmen and women endured extremes of weather, strange and perplexing diseases, rigorous labor, childbearing under the most adverse circumstances, sudden attacks from their enemies, and—perhaps worst of all—terrible loneliness.

Have you ever noticed that among the many designations and titles assigned to our Savior, "Pioneer," or "Trailblazer," is by far the one most calculated to stir the imagination?

For the record, it might interest you to know that the Greek word *archegos*—which has been variously translated as trailblazer or pioneer, leader, captain, and even author— appears just four times in the New Testament. In each of those four instances, it refers specifically to Jesus. In Acts 3:15 the apostle Peter charged that his fellow countrymen had killed the *archegos* of life. Further on in Acts 5:31, Peter referred to Jesus as the *archegos* who is at the Father's right hand. The writer of Hebrews bestowed on Him the title, the *archegos* of salvation (Hebrews 2:10), and later called Jesus the *archegos* of faith (Hebrews 12:2).

According to the Bible, we who are citizens of God's kingdom comprise a holy nation (1 Peter 2:9). This nation was pioneered by One who, in keeping with the descriptive passages above, forged at least three pathways while He was here on Earth: the way of life, the way of salvation, and the way of faith. Consequently, all who follow Him need never to fear getting lost or going astray. As a matter of fact, He is just ahead, calling out to any who would be His disciples, "Follow Me! I'll show you the way!"

> [16] *And I will bring the blind by a way that they knew not; I will lead them in paths that they have not known. I will make darkness light before them, and crooked*

things straight. These things will I do unto
them, and not forsake them. (Isaiah 42:16)

The Way of Life

The first, the way of life, may be the most
difficult path of the three. Most of us have discovered that living life is never a simple affair,
no matter what our circumstances. However,
no one knows what you are going through better than Jesus—you can count on it. If you
have examined the Record, you will have noted
that our Lord not only became hungry, thirsty,
and weary on occasion, but He experienced the
full range of human emotions that all of us do.
Indeed, this is one of the essential reasons He
came to Earth: He wanted to experience life
first hand, to taste what you taste and to feel
what you feel, to see what you see and hear
what you hear.

> [15] *For we do not have a High Priest who*
> *cannot sympathize with our weaknesses,*
> *but was in all points tempted as we are, yet*
> *without sin.* (Hebrews 4:15)

Because He knows your sorrows and has
suffered the onslaughts of the Enemy just as
you have, He is singularly qualified to intercede
on your behalf. When you think about it, who

else knows what you're going through better than the One who not only created you, but became just like you? And who else has access into the Judge's chambers like the Judge's own Son? It is even likely Jesus is there right now, pleading on your behalf!

> [34] *It is Christ who died, and furthermore is also risen, who is even at the right hand of God, who also makes intercession for us.*
> (Romans 8:34)

But, even more remarkable is the fact that, having experienced life from ground level and having been raised from the dead never to die again, Jesus has now resolved to live His life in and through you and me. In fact, this has been our destiny all along: to be His hands, His feet, His very body! Indeed, who else but Jesus—designated by God to be the Head of this living and vital organism—is able to equip us properly to live life in the midst of the myriad of decisions and details, trials and temptations, joys and sorrows, which we all face?

> [20] *I am crucified with Christ: nevertheless I live; yet not I, but Christ liveth in me: and the life which I now live in the flesh I live by the faith of the Son of God, who loved me, and gave himself for me.*
> (Galatians 2:20 KJV)

Our Trailblazer

The Way of Salvation

Jesus Christ, our Lord and Savior, also blazed this second path, that of salvation, for us. Yet, when I contemplate the fact that our Lord forged our route to salvation by way of the path of suffering, I never cease to be amazed. Scripture tells us that Jesus had to suffer to be perfected as our Savior.

> [8] *Though He was a Son, yet He learned obedience by the things which He suffered.*
> [9] *And having been perfected, He became the author of eternal salvation to all who obey Him.* (Hebrews 5:8–9)

I am sure that I am not the only person who has been puzzled by that Scripture. How could the second person of the Trinity have become more perfect than He already was? The plain fact is that the incarnate Word had never experienced being a savior before—at least, not the Savior who would save His people from their sins by becoming sin Himself (2 Corinthians 5:21)!

To be the Savior of the world meant being High Priest, Sacrifice, and Sin-Bearer simultaneously. As the appointed Savior of men, God the Son needed to become a man in order to be able to bear all that mankind bears: man's temptations, man's sufferings, and—most incredible of all—man's guilt, sin, and shame.

As Jesus willingly offered Himself up for our redemption, He provided the way for us to be forgiven of all our sin, to be cleansed of all our unrighteousness (1 John 1:9), and to *"become the righteousness of God in Him"* (2 Corinthians 5:21). Thus, in submitting to His heavenly Father, Jesus took upon Himself the task of forging the very path of salvation that had been declared of old:

> [10] *Go through, Go through the gates! Prepare the way for the people; Build up, Build up the highway! Take out the stones, Lift up a banner for the peoples!*
> [11] *Indeed the LORD has proclaimed to the end of the world:..."Surely your salvation is coming; behold, His reward is with Him, and His work before Him."* (Isaiah 62:10–11)

> [8] *A highway shall be there, and a road, and it shall be called the Highway of Holiness. The unclean shall not pass over it, but it shall be for others. Whoever walks the road...shall not go astray.* (Isaiah 35:8)

The Way of Faith

However, as we set out to follow the Lord on this *"Highway of Holiness,"* we soon discover that not only does it converge with the pathway of faith, but they are actually indistinguishable from each other. The fact is that life, salvation, and faith came together in one difficult and narrow way (Matthew 7:14) for our Lord, just as they do for us. The difference is that our Trailblazer forged a path where no man had ever gone before and—concerning the act of redemption through His death on the cross—where no one else could ever go.

From the outset, however, we must acknowledge that no book such as this could possibly consider even the most salient aspects of Jesus' walk of faith. Notwithstanding, we clearly find in Scripture that without faith it is impossible to please God (Hebrews 11:6), and that the Son brought joy to His Father's heart in all that He said and did (Matthew 3:17). Through Christ's example of pleasing the Father by walking and acting in complete trust, He forged the faith path on which He leads us.

The mark of a truly great leader is said to be that he will never ask someone to do what he is not willing to do himself. So, don't be anxious or get upset when the Lord speaks to your heart and says, "This, My disciple, is what I would like you to do today." In the common vernacular, He's already "been there, done that!" Jesus is keenly aware of all the obstacles and difficulties you will be facing, and so He has come up with a strategy that ensures your complete and unconditional success—when the goal is finally reached. All He asks is that you trust Him as He leads you.

Still, the difference between Christ's walk and ours is that Jesus experienced everything in life with an unwavering confidence in His heavenly Father. This aspect of Jesus' faith—cloaked in humility as it was—has always captivated me. So great was Jesus' trust in His Father's will for His life that He determined never to do anything without first getting His Father's approval. I suppose that as the second person of the Trinity He would have had every right to exercise His own will in all that He did. However, listen to what Jesus Himself said about the matter:

> [19] *Truly, truly, I say to you, the Son can do nothing of his own accord, but only what he sees the Father doing; for whatever he does, that the Son does likewise.*
>
> (John 5:19 RSV)

As a trusting child delights to depend on his father in all things, Jesus openly related that idea to His disciples without embarrassment, constraint, or equivocation. In so saying, He gave us the very pattern by which we are to live our lives on a day-by-day basis.

Our Trailblazer

The Pioneer of Faith

The Bible reveals within its pages aspects of Jesus' pilgrimage that are nothing short of phenomenal. For starters, let us consider our text: *"Jesus the pioneer...of our faith."* How is it that Jesus is called the Pioneer of Faith, especially when we take into account that *"faith cometh by hearing, and hearing by the word of God"* (Romans 10:17 KJV)? How could Jesus be our Pioneer when we consider the faith of those who came before Him, such as Moses, David, and even Abraham, the man known as "the father of the faithful"?

Did you know that all of us who walk by faith share something in common with those who have previously walked in faith, including father Abraham himself? Our faith is not in our faith, as many might lead us to believe. Faith always has an object, and the object of a Christian's faith is God, the One who was pleased to reveal Himself to us. Our faith—that is, our confidence, our trust—is in God and His disclosure of Himself to His creation, whether by way of His written revelation or by some other means.

The point is that faith comes about by hearing God speak to us and then putting our confidence and trust in what we have heard.

That is precisely what Abraham, Moses, and David did. And that is exactly what our Lord did! As a matter of fact, Jesus was the first to contemplate the ancient deliberations of the Trinity, as they were revealed to Him by the Spirit through the Scriptures, and then to put His convictions concerning those things that had been agreed upon into action! Because the preincarnate Word originated the plan in hope (Romans 8:20), and then the incarnate Son of Man fulfilled it, the Scriptures declare that He is *"the author and finisher of our faith"* (NKJV).

According to the Bible, in the council of the Godhead before the world was formed (1 Peter 1:20), it was determined that the Word would become flesh and dwell among men. It was agreed that He who is the Creator of all creatures great and small would Himself become *"the Lamb of God who takes away the sin of the world"* (John 1:29). This is underscored by the apostle John: *"the Lamb slain from the foundation of the world"* (Revelation 13:8).

Thus, the eternal Word—who did not count equality with God something to be held on to (Philippians 2:6)—submitted to the will of the Godhead and was born in the likeness of men. *"Being found in human form he humbled himself and became obedient unto death, even death on a cross"* (Philippians 2:8 RSV).

At the first, the design was only in the mind of the Godhead—something not yet played out in the space-time continuum—that man would be redeemed and even begotten of the Father. It was still to be recorded in the history books of humanity that all of creation would one day be gloriously set free from death and decay. But our Lord, by whom all things were spoken into existence, hoped for it (Romans 8:20–21); and then, in absolute confidence, He emptied Himself to be born in the likeness of men for the purpose of bringing it all about.

Consequently, as the object of our faith, Jesus Christ is the One who, in Himself, demonstrated what it means to have faith. You see, He was assured of things He was hoping for and convinced of things He did not yet see (Hebrews 11:1). Because He faithfully walked in God's plan, the Scriptures declare that it is Jesus, and Jesus alone, who is deserving of the title, *"the pioneer and perfecter of our faith."*

The Perfecter of Faith

In his classic, *In the Arena of Faith*, Erich Sauer quotes G. H. Lang as he paid tribute to Jesus our Lord as the *"perfecter of our faith"*:

> Thus, He originated the principle of faith (trust) in God, and He perfected the

development and display of faith by surrendering His original glory, by stepping
down to the state of manhood, by walking
on Earth as a dependent being, and above
all by surrendering Himself unto the
death of the cross. [1]

Faith was brought to its most perfect expression in Christ, but perfection is seldom
achieved without great cost and sacrifice—ask
any NFL quarterback, Olympic athlete, or
brain surgeon you might meet! However, can
mere words ever convey the supreme manifes-
tation of Jesus' faith in His Father—His sacrifice on the cross? No, because no one, not the
greatest theologian who has ever lived or the
most eloquent preacher who has ever occupied
a pulpit, has ever been able to truly count the
cost of Calvary. Yet, what we can try to do is
put things into perspective. In that way we
may better understand what it must have been
like for Jesus to die on our behalf.

What exactly took place on the cross?
What exactly was this sacrifice that was so
necessary in the plan of redemption that it
could not have been accomplished in any other
way? Why was it that it was in this death, the
death of the cross, that faith in God found its

---

[1] G. H. Lang, as quoted by Erich Sauer, *In the Arena
of Faith* (Grand Rapids: Eerdmans, 1955), 20.

purest expression? Surely, it was not just the physical act of being crucified, for were there not two thieves on either side of our Lord who were executed in essentially the same way? Indeed, thousands of victims of Rome's relentless enforcement of the *Pax Romana* had died on countless hills, just as Jesus had died.

Then, what was it about this particular death on this particular tree? For our answer, we must rely solely on the inspired Word:

> [13] *Christ redeemed us from the curse of the law, having become a curse for us—for it is written, "Cursed be every one who hangs on a tree."* (Galatians 3:13 RSV)

> [24] *He himself bore our sins in his body on the tree, that we might die to sin and live to righteousness. By his wounds you have been healed.* (1 Peter 2:24 RSV)

> [21] *For our sake* [the Father] *made* [Jesus] *to be sin who knew no sin, so that in him we might become the righteousness of God.* (2 Corinthians 5:21 RSV)

Did you realize that? He *"who knew no sin"* became sin for us. The purest of the pure, the most holy of all that is holy, the spotless Lamb of God who sought only to bless, heal, and redeem—this One willingly took upon Himself our sin, guilt, and shame on the cross!

He did not hold the transgressions of the most vile and filthy or the sins of the most wicked at arm's length. Instead, He embraced them as if they were His own!

And then, He died. Scripture declares that *"the wages of sin is death"* (Romans 6:23), and the one who sins must surely die. Thus, for our sakes, the One who never knew what it was to sin, literally—not figuratively or metaphorically, but literally—became sin on our behalf.

The consequence of sin is death—there are no exceptions in God's just judgment. But, we are not talking about death as by stoning or hanging or even the cruel death Jesus endured. Physical death, even the scandalous death of crucifixion, is not the issue here. Rather, what the Scriptures mean by *"even the death of the cross"* (Philippians 2:8) is the bitter cup of abhorrent destiny that Jesus, in earnest supplication, had not once, not twice, but three times implored His heavenly Father to remove (Matthew 26:39, 42, 44).

Gethsemane

Apparently, it was in the Garden of Gethsemane that Jesus fully comprehended what it would mean to bear the sins of the world in His own person. The realization hit Him with the force of two worlds colliding in space: for the first time in all of eternity, He would be separated from His Father. Loneliness of a sort never before imagined would become the bread of His affliction. He would be utterly divorced from the One who was the source of all genuine love, joy, and peace. How would He be able to endure being *"cut off from the land of the living"* (Isaiah 53:8)? He became well aware that on the cross there would be no comfort of the Father, no spiritual resources from which He would be allowed to draw upon, not even the hope of the dawning of a new day.

There would only be sin, indeed, the sin of all mankind, that would invade His soul as the foulest of cancers invades the body. Yet, far, far worse was the awful consequence of bearing those sins—death, death of a kind that only those who occupy the darkest regions of hades and inhabit the most foul habitations of hell know anything about. And so, His agonizing plea burst forth from His trembling lips: *"O My Father, if it be possible, let this cup pass from Me"* (Matthew 26:39).

But then, praise God, welling up from within His breaking heart came the expression of absolute assurance and confident trust that resulted in our very salvation: *"Nevertheless not My will, but Yours, be done"* (Luke 22:42)!

In Christ Jesus, faith had found its most articulate voice. Even as He went to the cross and experienced the agonizing pain of desertion, Christ held on to His faith in His heavenly Father with an unshakable grip. He humbly submitted to what His Father asked of Him and so perfected the way of faith.

Yes, such mysteries were first set into motion in the heavenlies, but the determination to carry them out, by the first Man to submit wholly to God, was made in Gethsemane. The decision to embrace our sins was made in that garden sanctuary. The result of that decision was Golgotha's stark tree.

Calvary

Thus, as Jesus hung helpless and alone on the cross, an inky, black shroud blanketed the land, turning the sun-filled midday into moonless night, as *the Lord...laid on Him the iniquity of us all* (Isaiah 53:6).

> [46] *About the ninth hour Jesus cried out with a loud voice, saying, "Eli, Eli, lama sabachthani?" that is, "My God, My God, why have You forsaken Me?"* (Matthew 27:46)

But no answer could be heard to our Savior's plaintive cry—only the echoes of His own lamentation. The heavens were silent as He bore the sins of the world in His own body on the tree. It was time to drink the vile dregs of the cup the Father had given Him.

It is only from our vantage point on this side of the cross that we can begin to grasp the painful reality of that haunting question, *"Why have You forsaken Me?"* Not only did our Savior have to bear our sins, He had to bear them alone. On the cross He was separated from the One who had guided His every step. And the loneliness and pain of bearing the sin of mankind brought about a perplexity of mind and distress of spirit never before known by man.

But now, let's see what the answer is.

> [4] *Surely he has borne our griefs and carried our sorrows; yet we esteemed him stricken, smitten by God, and afflicted.*
> [5] *But he was wounded for our transgressions, he was bruised for our iniquities; upon him was the chastisement that made us whole, and with his stripes we are healed.* (Isaiah 53:4–5 RSV)

Praise God! Christ conquered Golgotha rather than the other way around! Calvary is the end of the trail—the very means by which a holy nation has been conceived. *"It is finished!"* (John 19:30). Hallelujah! What a Savior!

The Path Jesus Walked Alone

In your mind's eye, imagine Jesus now as He picks up His sword to blaze a new trail. He goes on before us, not as one who sees and knows all, but as the very first Man who has ever truly trusted God in everything that He says and does.

See Him now as He trudges through the quicksand of a sin-sick, dying world, unhindered by the temptations that would suck Him into oblivion.

See Jesus now as He braves the storm of Satan's fury. How great is the blast from that Evil One who knows his time is short; at all costs and by any means, he must stop the Messiah before it is too late. Undaunted, our Lord presses on, although He is weary beyond description and long is the road that still lies before Him.

See Him now as the trail grows ever steeper. Mountains of adversity, misunderstanding, jealousy, and slander rise up before Him and threaten Him on every side. Yet He endures, despising the shame for the joy that is set before Him.

See Jesus now as He suffers the desert of desertion. Would-be fellow travelers have all forsaken Him. He is alone. Even His Father can comfort Him no longer, for the Son has taken upon Himself the transgressions of His people. They are like a mighty weight. How great is the burden Jesus must bear! Ever hotter grows the sun, draining Him of all of His strength and reserve. The judgment for sin is as a scorching wind ever beating upon Him. He stretches Himself out upon the sands of time. He thirsts, but no one can quench the despair of His loneliness. Distressed and disoriented, He cries aloud. Listen: *"Eli, Eli, lama sabachthani?...My God, My God, why have You forsaken Me?"*

Walking Together with Christ

Now, Christ invites us to walk the pathway that He cleared for us through His death, but He has not left us to fend for ourselves. He has promised, *"I will never leave you nor forsake you"* (Hebrews 13:5). As our humble Trailblazer, Jesus is always present to lead us down the convergent paths of life, salvation, and faith, just as He long ago assured us:

> [21] *To this you were called, because Christ suffered for you, leaving you an example, that you should follow in his steps.*
>
> (1 Peter 2:21 NIV)

> [16] *I will bring the blind by a way they did not know; I will lead them in paths that they have not known. I will make darkness light before them, and crooked things straight. These things will I do unto them, and not forsake them.* (Isaiah 42:16)

One man should love and honor one woman:
A bride-bed theirs alone
till life is done.

—Euripedes
Andromache, 426 B.C.

There are two sorts of constancy in love;
the one comes from the constant discovery
in our beloved of new grounds for love,
and the other comes from making it
a point of honor to be constant.

—La Rochefoucauld
Maxims, 1665

Chapter 9

Here Comes the Bride

They were married on New Year's Day because they wanted to begin the new year, and the rest of their lives, together. So much in love, they vowed on their wedding day that only death would part them. Their love for one another only grew as the days became years, and the years passed more quickly than either of them could have imagined. But, finally, inevitably, their days together drew to a close. As the time slipped by, they clung to each other even more closely. Neither wanted to leave the other, and they determined all the more that even death would not keep them apart.

The last day of their lives came on the last day of the year, the day before what would have been their sixty-ninth wedding anniversary. Demetris "Pete" and Elizabeth "Tot"

Davis died while lying in side-by-side beds at the Healthcare Nursing Home in Easley, South Carolina. Both ninety-one years old, they died within a heartbeat of each other. "The nurses think that Tot stopped breathing, and then they heard Pete make one gasp after that," their doctor reported. "It was almost simultaneous."

As devoted as Pete and Tot were to each other, it would take a lot more than love and devotion to explain the phenomenon of their death. It was almost as if they were one in spirit and body as well as in heart. But, of course, that is precisely the way it should have been. Their oneness should be something typical of marriages rather than an inspiring exception.

That was our Lord's intention from the beginning. As a matter of fact, it is His desire that every marriage of man and woman be a reflection of the relationship between His Son and the church. Put in another way, God wants us to be able to see in our marriages what is meant by the biblical declaration that Jesus is the Bridegroom and we are His bride.

Did you know that our Savior eagerly looked forward to a relationship of oneness with His church even before the world came into being? It was the plan of the Godhead all

along that the Word would one day become
flesh so that He could seek out, woo, and win
the one who would fulfill Him in every way,
His bride—a bride who eventually would become so beautiful and pure and lovely that He
would be willing to die for her.

Indeed, such would be the cost of His
yearning. Before the foundation of the world,
in the mind of God, Christ was crucified to
bring just such a thing about (Revelation 13:8).
It is for this reason that when Jesus looked
steadfastly toward Jerusalem and the cross He
had come to bear, He scorned any feelings of
shame that rose up within Him. Why? He
could do so because of *"the joy that was set before Him"* (Hebrews 12:2)! He was eagerly
looking forward to His most exciting dreams
coming true.

The Joy of Anticipation

Can you remember what it was like to anticipate the first day of summer vacation? The
anticipation itself was delicious. Can you recall
the time when you looked forward to your very
first date or the first time you ever drove a
car—all the preparation and daydreaming in-
volved, the eager expectation? Have you ever
worked up a sweat just thinking that the date

you have been planning for weeks might be the time when you would finally get to kiss the one you've had a crush on all semester?

There is something exquisitely wonderful about looking forward to a special event. It's a time to let your imagination go wild, to get butterflies in your tummy, and to be overwhelmed with roller-coaster emotions. Isn't it true that those times make up some of our most treasured memories? When something is especially valued and we anticipate taking part in it, an excitement invariably wells up in us. And that is exactly how God intended it!

This is only one of the reasons why entering into the intimacy of the marriage bed without the benefit of marriage invariably leads to disappointment. Every woman needs a sense of security before she can fully give of herself to her husband. That is why sexual intimacy outside of marriage is so frustrating: it can never be the complete, joyous, abandoned experience that our Lord meant it to be. The marriage bed brings a certain indefinable stability to the human psyche that alone allows us to fully enter into and enjoy the rich, varied blessings of an intimate relationship.

That is why the honeymoon ought to be the time for the most exciting moments ever experienced by the bride and groom: when new and overwhelming emotions are being shared for the first time, when a once-in-a-lifetime event is entered into with great anticipation, when the bride reserves herself for the one who has demonstrated by his holy restraint just how much he loves her. Then and only then will she be able to give herself to her husband without reservation. Needless to say, the groom has come to the point where his most passionate dreams are about to be realized, and just the anticipation of it all can set about a delirium of the most exquisite kind in him!

Now, recall that moment when Adam first beheld his bride and exclaimed, *"This at last is bone of my bones and flesh of my flesh"* (Genesis 2:23 RSV). What a classic example of expectations fulfilled!

Helpmates for Adam and for Christ

However, there is more to the story than Adam's expectations being met. God knew that Adam would need a *"help meet"* (Genesis 2:18 KJV) suitable for the author of the human race. Thus, He brought Eve forth directly from Adam's side. Unlike all other creatures of God's vast creation, Eve was not independently called forth into existence. No, God couldn't have made it any clearer: without Adam there could have been no Eve because she sprang forth directly from her husband. That is precisely why God looked on them as being *"one flesh"* (Genesis 2:24). After all, they were made of the same stuff!

This is the joyous enigma of planet Earth's first couple—and all couples since—when one equals two and two are really one! Even though for the rest of their lives they would function as two separate, distinct individuals, God would forevermore consider them as a single unit. From His divine perspective, they were one. Thus, we can comprehend His decree concerning all who would, from then on, be joined in holy matrimony:

> *24 Therefore a man shall leave his father and mother and be joined to his wife, and they shall become one flesh.* (Genesis 2:24)

The mystery remains even now. Although the man may come from a completely different cultural or sociological background than his beloved, or the woman may be decades younger than her husband, from God's point of view they are still *"one flesh."*

But, that isn't all the Bible says about the mysterious relationship between husbands and wives. The apostle Paul informs us that Adam and Eve's union serves as a type (a symbolic, yet real model that foreshadows a coming event or person) of that most blessed marriage of all, the union between Jesus Christ and His bride:

> ³¹ *"For this reason a man shall leave his father and mother and be joined to his wife, and the two shall become one flesh."*
> ³² *This is a great mystery, but I speak concerning Christ and the church.*
>
> (Ephesians 5:31–32)

Here we are informed that not only is the first man, Adam, a type of the Second Man, Jesus Christ, but that Adam and Eve are a type of Jesus and His bride. There is a very special reason why it is so important for us to see this connection. Recall once more how Eve was brought forth from Adam's side. Because of this, Adam could declare, *"This is now bone of my bones and flesh of my flesh"* (Genesis 2:23). When Adam awoke from his sleep, he no doubt was keenly aware of at least two changes: he finally had a helpmate for his needs, and he had a wound in his side to prove it!

Needless to say, it was not possible for Adam to leave his father and mother in order to hold fast to his wife, but such was Adam's dedication and devotion. "Eve is mine, and she is completely different from all of the other creatures of God's vast creation," he must have reflected. "She is actually a part of my very being, created especially to meet my needs. What a glorious, imaginative Creator to have so fashioned us!"

The Type Is Fulfilled in Christ

Now, let's discover the link between these two events: Adam getting a helpmate and Jesus getting a bride. The apostle John reported the following about the events that surrounded the death of our Husband, the Second Adam:

> ³² *Then the soldiers came and broke the legs of the first and of the other who was crucified with Him.*
> ³³ *But when they came to Jesus and saw that He was already dead, they did not break His legs.*
> ³⁴ *But one of the soldiers pierced His side with a spear, and immediately blood and water came out.*   (John 19:32–34)

If you are a part of the bride of Christ, I know that you will be as thrilled with the following discovery as I was when I made it. Did you know that in the Septuagint (LXX), which is a very early Greek translation of the Old Testament from the original Hebrew, the Greek word for *"side"* in Genesis 2:21 is identical to the word used here in John 19:34?

²¹ *And the LORD God caused a deep sleep to fall on Adam, and he slept; and He took of his side and closed up the flesh in its place.*
(Genesis 2:21, literal rendering of the LXX)

The Scripture records that God, in preparation for divine surgery, caused a deep sleep to fall upon the first man, Adam. Similarly, the Second Man, Jesus Christ, embraced the sleep of death itself in order that His bride might be brought forth to *"newness of life"* (Romans 6:4).

Further, just as the side of the first man was opened in order to accomplish the eternal purposes of God, so the side of Jesus, the Second Man, was pierced, and His blood shed, in order to bring His bride into existence:

²⁸ *...the church of God which He brought into existence by the act performed with His own blood.*
(Acts 20:28, author's translation)

However, our Lord was determined that even death would not keep us apart. He rose from the dead, demonstrating His great love for us. Such is His dedication and devotion. "I love you," He cries. "I have always loved you. It was necessary that I should die on Calvary, for without the shedding of My blood there could be no forgiveness of sins. But now you are washed; now you are as clean as the new-fallen snow. Through My death I have made you, My precious bride, truly beautiful, pure, and lovely. You are My virgin bride, *'bone of My bone and flesh of My flesh.'* My side was pierced—here is the wound to prove what I say—so that you, My bride, could be brought into existence without any spot or wrinkle. I have risen from the dead so that we can be together forever. We really are one, you know. No longer does the Father look upon us as separate and distinct from one another, for you are My body."

We Fulfill Our Lord

The most amazing facet of this brilliant diamond of God's grace is still to be seen. When God gave Eve to Adam as His supreme gift of love, it was due to the fact that Adam really needed her.

> [18] And the LORD God said, "It is not good that man should be alone; I will make him a helper suitable for him."
>
> (Genesis 2:18 NIV)

Adam could not have gotten along without Eve. The two of them, as a unit, would be able to accomplish more than Adam ever could have achieved alone. Eve fulfilled Adam; she completed him.

I have already spoken with affection about my Diane. Not only do I love my wife, but I need her. As a matter of fact, I don't know what I would do without her. She fulfills my every need as a man. She complements every aspect of my being, and that is especially true concerning my ministry. I thank God for my precious Diane, His great love-gift to me, and I intend to cherish her as long as God gives us breath.

According to the Scripture, that is exactly how our Lord looks upon us. What an extraordinarily humbling thought!

> [22] *And* [God] *put all things under* [Jesus'] *feet, and gave Him to be head over all things to the church,*
> [23] *which is His body, the fullness of Him who fills all in all.* (Ephesians 1:22–23)

Most of us probably don't have a problem with the fact that Jesus *"fills all"* things. He is not only the Answer, the Completion, the Zenith of the ages, but His very presence fulfills our every need. Yet, when we pause to consider the fact that Jesus looks on us as the one who fulfills His needs, the one who completes Him, it is almost too much for us to grasp.

I am persuaded that we, as individuals, have yet to comprehend just who we are from

God's perspective. Have you ever contemplated the idea that Jesus is courting you, that He intends to take you to be with Himself forever as His bride, and that He is anticipating the Wedding Supper of the Lamb even more than you are? Have you realized just how thoroughly He is committed to you? Are you able to verbalize the fact that Jesus really needs you?

Oh, what a Savior! Oh, what a Lord, this One whom we serve! How can we not be faithful to One who loves us so? He is coming again to be with His bride forever. He has asked us to wait for His return. He has even shared with us His vision for the future. Even now, He is preparing a honeymoon cottage, if you please, just for us, a place for us to call home.

> [2] *In My Father's house are many mansions; if it were not so, I would have told you. I go to prepare a place for you.*
> [3] *And if I go and prepare a place for you, I will come again and receive you to Myself; that where I am, there you may be also.*
> (John 14:2–3)

May we never adulterate our sacred vows as we wait patiently for His return. He is coming soon. Let us take the oil of the Spirit and make our lamps ready, for our Bridegroom is coming. Let the honeymoon begin!

A rock pile ceases to be a rock pile
the moment a single man contemplates it,
bearing within him the image of a cathedral.

—Saint-Exupery
Flight to Arras

Chapter 10

Like Oil upon the Head

*J*esus Christ—what familiar words. Sorry to say, they are all too familiar for some. Isn't it fascinating that those two words have affected the world in such diverse ways? How odd that for so many, *Jesus Christ* is the very phrase that epitomizes profanity.

How could such a thing have happened? How is it *"the name that is above every name"* (Philippians 2:9 NIV) has become the obscenity of choice? Why is it that men and women alike hurl those words from their lips like they were guided missiles? The name that was meant to bless has become the quintessential curse in the arsenal of a sin-sick, dying world. How ironic that He who voluntarily became a curse for mankind should bear the name that vile men now sling as a curse upon their fellows.

What surprises many Christians about the name is that *Jesus Christ* is not even Jesus' name! To be sure, *Jesus* is Jesus' name, which was assigned to Him by angelic proclamation even before He was born. Bible teachers like to point out that the name was derived from *Yeshua* (Joshua), which means "Jehovah is salvation." Even so, Jesus was a fairly common name, even as it is in many cultures today. So, there wasn't anything particularly significant about Jesus being named after one of the great heroes of the Hebrew faith. After all, He was, it was supposed, simply the promising young son of Joseph the carpenter.

No, what sets Jesus apart is a title, the title designated for Him by His followers when they declared, *"You are the Christ"* (Matthew 16:16). *Christ*, you see, was not originally a part of Jesus' name. The title *Christ* means "the Anointed One." To put it another way, the term *"the Christ"* is the New Testament equivalent of the term that Old Testament Jews used for *"the Messiah"* (Daniel 9:25 KJV).

By the time Jesus was on Earth, the term *Messiah* had taken on much significance in the culture. Remember Andrew's words when he located his brother: *"'We have found the Messiah' (which is translated, the Christ)"* (John 1:41). What Andrew meant by his excited cry spans generations of expectation and encompasses a heritage rich with symbolism.

Like Oil upon the Head

The Messiah, the Christ of God, would be as no other: ancient biblical prophecies maintained that only One could or would possess the office of the Anointed One. To be sure, others had been anointed before Jesus came. However, Jesus would be anointed *"more than [His] companions"* (Hebrews 1:9); the Christ would be anointed with *"the Spirit without measure"* (John 3:34 NAS).

Set Apart unto God

To be a part of that limited company of anointed ones was something unparalleled in human experience. To be anointed was to be the recipient of that to which only a few could make a claim. To be anointed meant being set apart, solely dedicated to the purposes of God. To be anointed was to be placed in a position of privilege and blessing. To be anointed was to be noted as one singularly favored by the Lord.

In addition, to be anointed meant to be saturated with oil—doused, drenched, soaked with oil—sticky, messy, clinging oil. Over and down the head it would flow, into the ears and into the nose. Down it would drip, into the beard and into one's clothes. When someone was anointed in those days, he knew it. It was meant to be an occasion never to be forgotten.

However, the occasion itself soon paled when compared to the glory of what the anointing stood for. The pouring of the oil on the head symbolized a far greater anointing from above. As the oil dripped down upon the recipient's head and seeped into his eyes, no matter how tightly closed, the candidate was reminded that from that moment on his eyes were to be dedicated to God's purposes. So, too, were his ears and lips anointed, as well as his hands and feet. All of his members were set apart and consecrated for the glory of God. The Most Holy Spirit of the living God could now be poured forth upon that one as *"the oil of gladness"* (Hebrews 1:9). When the Spirit of God came upon a man, he would no longer be as he once had been. He would be empowered to do that which was far beyond his own ability. When God's Spirit did descend, men were inevitably stunned by the consequences.

Prophets, Priests, and Kings

Prophets, of course, were anointed. So, too, were priests, as were kings. Of course, we are referring here to Jewish prophets, priests, and kings, which narrows the list considerably. You may recall a few notable exceptions—for instance, the Lord God giving the prophet Elijah specific instructions to anoint Hazael to be king of Syria, as recorded in 1 Kings 19:15—but on the whole, those anointed for such an office were rather few and far between.

The reason there were so few anointed, though, had very little to do with the goodness of those so favored. For example, look at the case of King Saul. He was God's anointed—raving mad, but anointed. The reason Saul had been anointed with oil was not because he was Saul, but because he had been chosen by God to be the king of Israel. If the selected king had been someone other than Saul, then that other someone would have been anointed instead of Saul. Nevertheless, it was Saul who was singled out to be, for a time, God's political representative on the face of the earth.

Israel was the nation God had set apart for His purposes. The leader of that nation would need supernatural wisdom and guidance to fulfill a supernatural agenda. These were not just any people who stood in need of a king; these were God's people. Their king couldn't be just any king; their king had to be one who was empowered by God Himself to fulfill the destiny of the tribes of Israel.

The character and even the personality of that king might change throughout the course of his lifetime, but a king didn't stop being king because he had lost faith with the people or even with his God. Kings in those days were not just kings for a day. Saul wasn't always sane, but he was appointed to be the king of Israel until the day he died.

In the same way, God's appointment and anointing of the priests and prophets were for life, without regard to the behavior or character of those chosen. *"For the gifts and the calling of God are irrevocable"* (Romans 11:29).

Do you recall which prophet was immortalized in Scripture as having been found without fault in his character? Read this as a reminder:

[3] *Then this Daniel distinguished himself above the governors and satraps, because an excellent spirit was in him; and the king gave thought to setting him over the whole realm.*
[4] *So the governors and satraps sought to find some charge against Daniel concerning the kingdom; but they could find no charge or fault, because he was faithful; nor was there any error or fault found in him.* (Daniel 6:3–4)

However, later Daniel himself wrote,

[20] *Now while I was speaking, praying, and confessing **my** sin and the sin of my people Israel, and presenting my supplication*

> *before the LORD my God for the holy moun-*
> *tain of my God.* (Daniel 9:20)

Even this man, who was seen by outsiders as being faultless, had failings and weaknesses, and he recognized his own sinful state. It was not Daniel's perceived purity that enabled him to prophesy and interpret dreams, but God's supernatural anointing.

Elijah was another prophet whom we tend to view as being spiritually greater or more holy than we are, especially when we look at all of the miracles God worked through him. Yet, in the context of teaching about prayer, James wrote of him:

> [16] *Confess your faults one to another, and pray one for another, that ye may be healed. The effectual fervent prayer of a righteous man availeth much.*
> [17] *Elias was a man subject to like passions as we are, and he prayed earnestly that it might not rain: and it rained not on the earth for a space of three years and six months.*
> [18] *And he prayed again, and the heaven gave rain, and the earth brought forth her fruit.* (James 5:16–18 KJV)

Just like us, Elijah was subject to overwhelming emotions and human nature. Having humiliated and eliminated 450 prophets of Baal, and then having prayed for the rains to resume after the drought, he received a death threat from a woman and hightailed it out into the wilderness. So terrified was he that he forgot God's miraculous power and prayed to die. (See 1 Kings 18 and 19.) Again, the Scriptures make it clear that the miracles Elijah performed were not the result of his sterling character or unwavering faith, but because God chose to anoint him.

Whether or not a man got up on the wrong side of the bed had nothing to do with whether or not God used his mouth that day. (For a real eye opener, read the story of Balaam and his talking beast of burden that is described in chapter 22 of Numbers.) I could go on, but I hope the point has been well established: anointed people are ordinary people, *"subject to like passions as we are,"* who do extraordinary things precisely because they are anointed.

Jesus, the Anointed Messiah

What was it like, Lord Jesus, when You emptied yourself of being in the form of God? What was it like for You to find Yourself wrapped in human flesh? As Joseph taught You the Torah and as Mary shared with You the secrets of her heart, what did You contemplate in Your mind? As you grew in grace and knowledge, did questions ever arise in Your heart? Was the reassuring witness of Your heavenly Father's Spirit all you needed to have the confidence that You were, indeed, the only begotten Son of God? Were You aware from Your childhood of why You had come to dwell among us? When did You first realize that You were the promised Messiah, the Christ? When did it first occur to You that You had been born to die?

The Name above All Names

Jesus Christ. How we ought to pray that these two words, so linked together, may become words that are truly spoken to bless in this world, and not to curse, as they are so often used today.

Jesus: Savior. Born to die that we may live.
Christ: Anointed One. Our Prophet, Priest, and King.

The Peculiar Anointing of Jesus

Jesus was born Jesus; it was the name given to Him at His birth. However, Jesus had not been *the Christ* from birth. He became the Anointed One shortly after His thirtieth birthday, immediately following His baptism in the Jordan River by His cousin John.

> [16] *When He had been baptized, Jesus came up immediately from the water; and behold, the heavens were opened to Him, and He saw the Spirit of God descending like a dove and alighting upon Him.*
>
> (Matthew 3:16)

It was to this very event that Jesus alluded when He said,

> [18] *The Spirit of the LORD is upon Me, because He has anointed Me to preach the gospel to the poor; He has sent Me to heal the brokenhearted, to proclaim liberty to the captives and recovery of sight to the blind, to set at liberty those who are oppressed;*
> [19] *To proclaim the acceptable year of the LORD.* (Luke 4:18–19)

However, note, if you will, that oil itself was never used in Jesus' anointing. It wasn't until His life and ministry were drawing to a close that He was finally anointed with oil. His heavenly Father didn't wait for one of us to become aware that He was indeed the Messiah. He baptized His Son in the Holy Spirit without even consulting the religious leaders of the day. God Himself poured forth His Spirit without measure upon His only begotten Son to usher in the era of grace. No, it was not until the end of His ministry that Jesus was actually

Like Oil upon the Head

anointed with oil. Perhaps you remember the scene:

> ⁶ *And when Jesus was in Bethany at the house of Simon the leper,*
> ⁷ *a woman came to Him having an alabaster flask of very costly fragrant oil, and she poured it on His head as He sat at the table.* (Matthew 26:6–7)

Here was a woman who definitely knew what she was doing but obviously didn't know what she was doing, all at the same time!

> ¹² *For in pouring this fragrant oil on My body, she did it for My burial.*
> ¹³ *Assuredly, I say to you, wherever this gospel is preached in the whole world, what this woman has done will also be told as a memorial to her.* (Matthew 26:12–13)

What a fitting memorial for an unnamed woman who might otherwise have never been noticed by the recorders of history.[1] But this woman, unlike the apostles and disciples who had walked daily with their Lord, felt compelled to proclaim that He was the Messiah in

---

[1] While it has often been surmised that this woman was Mary from John's gospel (see John 12:1–8), a careful reading of the Scriptures shows that the woman's identity was deliberately kept anonymous in Matthew's record of this unique event.

dramatic fashion. She rejoiced when she realized she was to be in the company of the long-awaited Messiah, and so she boldly took it upon herself to act out the role of the anointing vessel. She, through her fearless gesture, would give testimony that this Jesus was, indeed, the Lord's Anointed. But, as she poured forth her treasured oil upon His head, she had no idea what Jesus alone knew: soon He would be put to death. How could she have known the mystery that only in dying could Jesus become the Christ, the Messiah, of all nations and for all generations?

Thank you, dear lady, for recognizing on our behalf who Jesus was and is. Thank you for accomplishing at the end of His ministry what the religious leaders of the day should have done at the very beginning: acknowledging the Messiah by pouring forth the oil of gladness upon His head.

What Anointing with Power Implies

Once again I direct you to the Scriptures about Christ's humility. *"The Word became flesh"* (John 1:14). He who was in the form of God took upon Himself the form of a slave (Philippians 2:7). He who once rode the winds (Psalm 18:10) became an embryo in His mother's womb—which many in our day would have simply chosen to abort, conveniently labeling the pregnancy as "a mistake."

Obviously, newborns are not known for healing the deaf or raising the dead; they do well to roll over by themselves. And so it was with our Lord. He emptied Himself to be born an infant. As He grew to manhood, He waited on His heavenly Father to equip Him for the ministry to which He had been called. Still, the wonderful thing about being truly empty is that there is nothing left to get in the way of being filled! What better candidate for the office of the Anointed One could have existed?

> [34] *For He whom God has sent speaks the words of God, for God does not give* [Him] *the Spirit by measure.*
> [35] *The Father loves the Son and has given all things into His hand.*   (John 3:34–35)

> [36] *You know the word which God sent to the children of Israel, preaching peace through Jesus Christ....*
> [38] *how God anointed Jesus of Nazareth with the Holy Spirit and with power, who went about doing good and healing all who were oppressed by the devil, for God was with Him.*   (Acts 10:36, 38)

*Would that I could discover truth
as easily as I can uncover falsehood.*

—Cicero
De Natura Deorum

Chapter 11

The Word of God Redux

Picture this: a youthful face framed by a head of hair whiter than your great-grandma's; bronzed feet of statuary that support an otherwise human-looking form of flesh and bones; blinding, supernatural light shooting forth from unblinking eyes; and a dagger-like weapon of bright, burnished metal that protrudes from the mouth of this unearthly visitor.

Is this Robo-Cop IV, the latest look in Terminators, or the imagination of a twelve-year-old child played out in virtual reality? It is none of the above. But, I hope that you recognize it as the vision described by the apostle John in the book of Revelation—John's vision of Jesus, God the Word, after His ascension into the heavenlies!

¹² *Then I turned to see the voice that spoke with me. And having turned I saw seven golden lampstands,*
¹³ *and in the midst of the seven lampstands One like the Son of Man, clothed with a garment down to the feet and girded about the chest with a golden band.*
¹⁴ *His head and hair were white like wool, as white as snow, and His eyes like a flame of fire;*
¹⁵ *His feet were like fine brass, as if refined in a furnace, and His voice as the sound of many waters;*
¹⁶ *He had in His right hand seven stars, out of His mouth went a sharp two-edged sword, and His countenance was like the sun shining in its strength.*
¹⁷ *And when I saw Him, I fell at His feet as dead. But He laid His right hand on me, saying to me, "Do not be afraid; I am the First and the Last."* (Revelation 1:12–17)

Obviously, this vision of Jesus as the ascended Word of God really aroused the apostle John's attention. However, what piques my interest the most is that the voice John heard was associated with a sword protruding from the Messiah's mouth. Of course, if we have taken the time to compare this vision with other passages of Scripture, we have discovered the meaning of this startling symbol of the sword: it represents nothing less than

God's penetratingly powerful words coming forth from the mouth of the One who had been crucified, but who rose again, and who is now at the right hand of the Father.

What is as sharp as a two-edged sword yet as thunderous as an ocean's waves relentlessly pounding upon the shore? When the apostle John heard the voice of Jesus, he testified that it was *"as the sound of many waters"* (Revelation 1:15). As the waves crashed unceasingly upon the craggy cliffs of Patmos, so the sound of his Master's words came flooding into John's consciousness. He could not help but perceive the clear, unmistakable words of the Lord of the universe.

Jesus Speaks Today

Even above the tumult that wells up around us in our day and age, our Lord Jesus desires to speak to us just as powerfully and authoritatively as He did to His apostle John back then. Has Jesus spoken into your heart lately? "But, how?" you may ask. "How does Jesus speak today? I've never heard a roar like thunder; I've never even heard the faintest of whispers." Be assured that if you are willing to be His disciple, He longs to speak to you this very hour. I would stake my life on it!

Sometimes our Lord wants to speak to us in a very intimate way, just as He did with His disciples when they walked with Him along the dusty roads of Galilee. At other times He may speak to us sternly as a father might speak to a wayward child or as a commander might speak to his troops. Sometimes His words may bring a stinging rebuke, sometimes a note of comfort or cheer. Sometimes He may speak as a friend, sometimes as a teacher. Sometimes He may speak of the future, sometimes of the past, but always He speaks with words that find their mark.

"My sheep hear My voice, and I know them, and they follow Me" (John 10:27). Can you hear His voice? Listen carefully, for our Shepherd can still be heard calling to His lambs.

But how can we be sure that it is truly Jesus' voice we're hearing? How do we know it isn't the siren songs of those who would lure us to certain destruction? What if our pathways lead us down into the murky depths of deception? Worse, what if we are self-deceived? What is to keep us from falling headlong into currents of confusion? What safeguards are there in this age where everything is relative—irreverently and irrelevantly relative? The answer is now, as it was then, the security of that *"sharp two-edged sword"* (Revelation 1:16). For those of us in this generation, who are so far removed from the direct counsel of the original apostolic band, we have *"the sword of the Spirit"* (Ephesians 6:17), better known to us as the Bible, the written Word of God.

> [16] *Out of His mouth went a sharp **two-edged sword**.* (Revelation 1:16)

> [12] *For the word of God is living and powerful, and sharper than any **two-edged sword**, piercing even to the division of soul and spirit, and of joints and marrow, and is a discerner of the thoughts and intents of the heart.* (Hebrews 4:12)

> [17] ***The sword of the Spirit**, which is the word of God.* (Ephesians 6:17)

Look carefully at the above Scriptures and understand this mystery: the Bible—that is, the written Word of God—is in reality just as much an extension of Jesus' person as the sword that John saw protruding from Jesus' mouth. He who existed in the beginning as the Word of God faithfully spoke God's words while He sojourned on Earth. Those words have now been miraculously conveyed to us in written form by the effective working of the Holy Spirit. (See especially John 14:10–26.) In other words, the relationship between that sacred text we call the Holy Bible and its Author is more intimate than many of us may have imagined.

Our Only Sure Standard of Truth

Precisely because God's written Word is an extension of Jesus Christ, we can count on it being absolutely true. Not only that, it is also the only surefire way that we have on the face of this earth to check the validity of any other medium through which God may choose to make Himself known today.

What I mean to say is this: whether our Lord speaks to us intimately through dreams and visions or through the counsel of godly men and women, whether by way of angelic visitations or through the witness of God's Spirit in the inner man, we must never allow our subjective experiences to be the interpreters of God's Word. It must always be the other way around. Our emotions may cloud the issue, but we can be certain the Bible will always be objective in its declarations. Our motives may skew the interpretation of a dream or a parent's advice, but the Bible will never throw anything at us obliquely. That is why we must always interpret our experiences in the light of

God's invariable and unchanging revelation. The standard by which all subjective experiences are to be judged can be none other than God's written Word, the *Logos*, the Bible.

Yet, in so saying, we must quickly take note that nowhere in John's vision, or anywhere else in the Scriptures for that matter, are we encouraged to idolize *"the sword."* Believers are never exhorted to venerate or worship the Bible, as sacred as it is.

There really isn't any contradiction in what I have said. Consider it this way for a moment: just as our physical tongues serve us in communicating our thoughts to others, so the *"two-edged sword"* that proceeds from the mouth of Jesus, now in written form, is how He chooses to express Himself in this era of grace. Yes, my tongue is alive, but if it were to be cut off from me, it would become a dead and useless thing. In other words, my tongue has no meaning or purpose apart from me. Because I live, it has life. The bottom line is simply this: because Jesus lives, the Bible is!

Discerning Truth from Error

But there is yet another factor to take into account as we consider our Lord's primary way of speaking to the hearts and minds of His own today. You're probably painfully aware that people can and do interpret the Bible to make it say whatever they want. Sadly, there are more than a few Jim Joneses or David Koreshs out there.

So, how can anyone be absolutely sure that the Bible has been allowed to say what it means? I suggest that you ask yourself the following simple questions before you are ever tempted to accept some new idea as doctrine or an unusual interpretation of God's written Word as truth:

- Is what is being preached or taught in line with the character and ways of a pure and righteous God?
- Does it bring you closer to His holiness and inspire you to walk in holiness?
- Does it bring glory and honor and praise to Jesus, or does the emphasis of the teaching primarily focus on you, the believer, or another person?
- Would an outsider who enters your church or assembly think you are crazy because of what you are being asked to put into practice, or is it more likely he or she would become convicted that God Almighty is really in your midst?
- Finally, if this "new" idea were to be submitted to the church universal—the

community of believers-at-large, as opposed to some local gathering of possibly self-deceived individuals—could it bear up under the discerning judgment of those who are subject to the Spirit of Truth and have thus proven themselves as trustworthy leaders in the body of Christ?

Also keep in mind these Scriptures as guidelines:

[20] *Knowing this first, that no prophecy of Scripture is of any private interpretation,*
[21] *for prophecy never came by the will of man, but holy men of God spoke as they were moved by the Holy Spirit.*
(2 Peter 1:20–21)

[29] *Let two or three prophets speak, and let the others judge.* (1 Corinthians 14:29)

Isn't it wonderful to know that, by following a few simple guidelines established by our Lord in advance, He is able to keep us from the bondage of error and false teaching just as surely as He is able to deliver us from the shackles of sin!

This, of course, is based upon the assumption that you truly want to know God's Word, and therefore His will, for your life. None of the tests listed above will mean a thing unless you do. There is only one way that God's Spirit can bear witness with your spirit (Romans 8:16) and thereby give you the confidence that what you are receiving is actually of Him: this can only occur when your heart is in tune with His.

This is borne out by our Lord Himself, as recorded in the seventh chapter of the gospel of John. There we find a situation where certain Jews challenged Jesus about His teachings. The implication of their questioning was that His teachings were not from God at all. Jesus knew, however, what was really going on. His listeners knew neither God's will nor His heart, for if they had, they would have certainly known that Jesus was His Anointed Prophet. Recall how Jesus responded to their challenge:

> [17] *If any man's will is to do* [God's] *will, he shall know whether the teaching is from God or whether I am* [merely] *speaking on my own authority.* (John 7:17 RSV)

What blessed assurance for the disciple of Christ, straight from the lips of the Savior! And so, dear reader, if you have truly submitted your will to your heavenly Father, you can know today whether what is being taught is truly of Him, even as in those times.

The Word of God Redux

The Paradox

"What does all of this have to do with the humility of our Lord?" you may well ask. Well, when you think about it, just about everything. Ask yourself this question, To whom has our Lord entrusted this marvelous treasure of His Word, this extension of Himself, as it were, but to you and me? Who would have ever dreamed that He would have given this gift to none other than believers like you and me? We who are so very human—I am, at least—so error-prone in every area of life and living. That can be a very dangerous state of affairs, indeed!

Do you remember how, for many generations, God entrusted the Old Testament revelation of Himself to the religious leaders of that age and how most of them lost sight of its immeasurable value? How sad it is that the same thing is being repeated in so many circles of God's kingdom today. Nevertheless, our Lord has commissioned us to be stewards of its incalculable treasures. Now let me ask you, Why do you suppose He takes so great a chance with such fallible people as us?

As we look around, it should be painfully clear that we certainly need the Word of God as never before. That is precisely why the Lord went to such extraordinary lengths to preserve it for this time! The Word of God is to be to the soul and spirit what physical sustenance is to the body. For the believer, certainly, it is to be like manna, our daily bread. Moreover, it is a finely polished mirror that gives us a faithful reflection of who we really are, whether in Adam or whether in Christ. Additionally, countless multitudes have testified that the Bible has been a healing balm that soothes the nerves and calms the soul, bringing comfort in the midst of life's greatest pains and sorrows.

So, there is little doubt that we need the Word of God as never before, but is that reason enough for the Lord of creation to entrust it to the likes of you and me? Wouldn't it have been far better if He had, for example, committed it to the angels to do with as they saw fit? It seems so to our way of thinking. Nevertheless, He relegated it to us.

Jesus, Our Big Brother

What does that tell you about the One whom we serve? What a Savior! What a Lord! He became a man to remain a man forever in order that He might become *"the firstborn among many brethren"* (Romans 8:29). In other words, He did what He did because He delights in being our Brother—our big Brother who watches over and takes care of His family; our big Brother who wants to encourage us; our big Brother who wants to impart to us the confidence that as we trust the Father, we, too, can accomplish everything that God has called us to do. Our Brother has committed Himself to us completely and unreservedly. He not only loves us, but He likes us and desires our company and fellowship forever—yours and mine!

To top it all, He gives us the opportunity of being stewards over the very things that He suffered and died for! We are His appointed managers of the mysteries of heaven and Earth. He entrusts not only His Word, but His Spirit, His reputation, His very being, to His blood-bought family.

Yes, the Word of God still sets the captive free, and by its radiance countless paths are being illumined. God's Word can make even the simplest of men and women to be as wise as Solomon. And wise men still seek that One who humbly chooses to introduce Himself through the pages of a Book, a Book held and treasured by one of His little brothers or sisters, one of His grateful siblings who has experienced His presence and power.

[23] *Having been born again, not of corruptible seed but incorruptible, through the word of God which lives and abides forever,*

[24] Because *"All flesh is as grass, and all the glory of man as the flower of the grass. The grass withers, and its flower falls away,* [25] *"But the word of the LORD endures forever." Now this is the word which by the gospel was preached to you.* (1 Peter 1:23–25)

The best way to see divine light is to put out thy own candle.

—Thomas Fuller, D.D.

Chapter 12

Comparing Lights

I'll never forget Charlie. Charlie was a student who attended Northern Arizona University while I was the pastor of a church near the campus in Flagstaff. Charlie had been totally blind since birth, but he wasn't handicapped—at least, not to hear Charlie tell it. It seemed that Charlie did just about everything that anyone else did, and then some. Life for Charlie was just one exciting challenge after another. He enjoyed swimming, horseback riding, hiking, and even going to basketball games, as I recall.

I do vividly remember one day when we went on an outing together to Lake Havasu. As the two of us were paddling about in our little rental canoe, Charlie stunned me by confidently asking, "We're going under a bridge now, aren't we?"

"As a matter of fact, we are, but how did you know?" I mumbled, almost embarrassed to be asking such an obviously foolish question. Charlie told me how he had sensed the change in temperature as we entered the cooler region where the shadow of the bridge played upon the surface of the water. "Not to mention," he added, "that every sound became different when we went underneath the bridge."

As Charlie explained how he enjoyed his surroundings by sensing things that I didn't, I began to realize just how much I had taken for granted the one sense he had never known.

Eyes to See and Light to See By

What would it be like to live in utter darkness? What would it be like never to see the promise of a new day as the night gives way to a radiant sunrise? Can you imagine what it would mean to you if you never saw the sparkling white of newly fallen snow, the azure-blue of a placid lake, the gradients of green in a rolling hillside, the beauty of a sunset reflected in a loved one's eyes—or, for that matter, never saw your beloved's eyes? If you can't answer these questions, be grateful.

The eye—how extraordinary is its craftsmanship! Yet, without light it would exist for nothing, because nothing can be seen without light, no matter how healthy or proficient that most delicate of organs. Vision cannot be envisioned without light, and, simply put, color is the prismatic character of light. Without light, everything would not only be colorless, everything would be utterly dark, always. What would life be like without light? Aesthetically, unimaginable. Biologically, impossible. Biblically, unthinkable.

"Then God said, 'Let there be light'; and there was light" (Genesis 1:3), light for seeing, light for growing, light for living, light for glowing.

A Refresher Course in Physics

How extraordinary is this opulent display of God's handiwork, this phenomenon we call light![1] To this day, no one has been able to comprehend it. Did you know that light is by far the greatest mystery of the physical universe? Our most celebrated thinkers have yet to fathom light's characteristics. Our most distinguished scientists are still baffled by its properties. Without light nothing can exist

---

[1] For reasons of practicality, the general term "light" will sometimes represent the entire electromagnetic spectrum.

that does exist, yet no one who exists is able to resolve light's secrets. How strange it is that the basic element of modern-day physics remains without even elementary definition!

For starters, just consider the speed of light. If, from a stationary position, one were to measure the velocity of light, the results would be precisely 186,282 miles per second. Now, someone might suppose that if he were to travel toward the source of that light at, let's say, the tremendous speed of ten thousand miles per second and then measure its velocity, he would get a completely different result. The truth of the matter is, though, it would still measure exactly 186,282 miles per second. The result would also be the same if we were to measure the speed of a light beam while traveling away from its source. Although it seems logical to think the measurement would be different, the observer's movement has absolutely no effect on the speed of light, even though it does on the measurement of time. Why? As the old saying goes, God only knows.

Another very perplexing characteristic of light is that light slows down as it passes through a dense medium such as glass or water, yet it will resume its original speed once it has reentered the atmosphere—and without anyone giving it a little push along the way.

Comparing Lights

Let a physicist try to explain that! Nothing else in all the known universe acts quite this way. And we're not talking here about just certain kinds of light, such as light that emanates from a powerful source such as the sun. Light from a flashlight or a candle behaves the same way.

Let's take a look at one more property of light that befuddles today's best minds: the nature of light's propagation—that is, how light travels from its source to its destination. The reason it is such a puzzle is that the propagation of light does not always act in the same manner. Sometimes light behaves as if it were being carried along by waves from one place to another, but sometimes it acts as if it were being propelled much like particles shot from a gun. Nothing else in creation behaves in such a dualistic fashion. It's enough to drive a well-meaning physicist out of his mind!

God Is Light

Remember that previously we learned that *"God is light"* (1 John 1:5). Before you jump to any conclusions, let me make it clear that the Bible never asserts that the omnipresent Lord of the universe is equivalent to what we perceive as physical light. After all, no matter how wonderfully unique it may be, light is but the inanimate creation of our Creator. As God Himself declares,

> [7] *I form the light and create darkness....I, the LORD, do all these things.* (Isaiah 45:7)

Nevertheless, *"God is light."* How is that so? Just as the temple, the priesthood, the sacrificial system, the holy days, and so on, all served as shadows and types of a greater spiritual reality, so it is with the phenomenon we call light. Physical light is but a type of the very essence of God. In other words, the Bible declares that God is that Greater Light who dwells in the light of His own glory!

> [16] *Who alone has immortality, dwelling in unapproachable light, whom no man has seen or can see, to whom be honor and everlasting power. Amen.* (1 Timothy 6:16)

> [17] *Every good gift and every perfect gift is from above, and comes down from the Father of lights, with whom there is no variation or shadow of turning.* (James 1:17)

The Bible declares that the time will come when the sun and moon will no longer exist, because there will be no more need of those lesser lights. The Scriptures reveal that in that blessed day, the glory of the Lord will be the only light we'll need:

Comparing Lights

[19] *The sun shall no longer be your light by day, nor for brightness shall the moon give light to you; but the LORD will be to you an everlasting light, and your God your glory.*
(Isaiah 60:19)

[23] *The city had no need of the sun or of the moon to shine in it, for the glory of God illuminated it. The Lamb is its light.*
(Revelation 21:23)

An Overdue Explanation

Let's stop and rest for a moment or two. I have no desire either to wear you down with relevant facts of physics or to quote Scripture after Scripture, even if they are related by a common theme. What I want to do is punctuate this work on the humility of our Lord by demonstrating, by way of contrasting lights, the difference between our Savior's first state and His last.

So, let's return to the Genesis account of the beginning that we have been referring to throughout our study:

[1] *In the beginning God created the heavens and the earth.*
[2] *The earth was without form, and void; and darkness was on the face of the deep. And the Spirit of God was hovering over the face of the waters.*

³ *Then God said, "Let there be light"; and there was light.* (Genesis 1:1–3)

Now recall that other chronicle, the apostle John's commentary on Genesis found in the first chapter of his gospel. This is the way the beloved disciple, inspired by the Holy Spirit, refers to the account in Genesis:

¹ *In the beginning was the Word, and the Word was with God, and the Word was God.*
² *He was in the beginning with God....*
⁹ *That was the true Light which gives light to every man coming into the world.*
(John 1:1–2, 9)

Comparing Lights

How triumphant must have been the sound of that first fiat: *"Let there be light!"* With that simple decree, God's great plan was set in motion. How extraordinary must the result have been! A glorious effusion of light poured forth with no one to see it but the heavenly hosts. How the excitement of expectation must have grown with the realization that the stage was finally set and that God's scheme of begetting children was finally going to come to pass!

The brightness of the glory of that first light must have been overwhelming in its advent. How magnificent must have been that primordial glow, that sublime splendor in which all of creation was soon to be bathed! Of course, Moses was not there to witness that surpassing display first hand, but his baptized imagination, guided by God's Spirit, accurately recorded the event: *"Then God said, 'Let there be light'; and there was light"* (Genesis 1:3).

But, as the apostle John took up his pen to write, so many millennia later, he did so with a clarified perspective as well as a greater understanding. John's eyes, mind, and heart had been diverted by a far greater Light! He had seen with his own eyes a glory so far greater than the dawn of creation that the former, lesser light languished by comparison. It was as if John had witnessed a celestial eclipse of such magnitude that he would never be able to see anything again in quite the same way. All else faded when compared to the splendor of Jesus' majestic appearing. So, he wrote, *"the true Light which gives light to every man"* (John 1:9).

By *"the true Light"* John did not mean true as opposed to false, but true Reality by which all other lights are to be measured: Jesus is truly the Light of the World. Indeed, by His light men are enabled to see things as they really are! The Word of God became the Light of the World to bring illumination to a people dwelling in darkness. Furthermore, that Light of lights is so bright and powerful, no one who is truly seeking the truth or the light can possibly miss the way!

The Same, Yet Different

We have yet to see the humility of our precious Savior in becoming the Light of the World, however. For that aspect we must carefully examine a previously cited text: *"The city had no need of the sun or of the moon to shine in it, for the glory of God illuminated it. The Lamb is its light"* (Revelation 21:23).

Now, to the person who reads English translations of the Bible, there may be nothing unusual about the statement that *"the Lamb is its light,"*[2] assuming, of course, that the reader is familiar with John's use of the term *"Lamb"* as a priestly way of referring to Jesus: *"The Lamb of God who takes away the sin of the world"* (John 1:29). No, what is interesting here in Revelation is the original word John chose to use for light. John did not employ the

---

[2] Literally, *"Its lamp is the Lamb,"* as translated in the RSV, NAS, etc. The original word means a movable light source such as a candle or oil-burning lamp.

usual Greek term, *phos,* that he had used previously in referring to the Lord. Rather, here he used a completely different term for light from the one found in his gospel. This Greek word *luchnos* actually indicates a portable lamp!

"What of it?" you may well ask. The point that John made in using this unusual term is one that we English readers should be made aware of: even though the light that will illuminate that fair city is nothing less than the glory of God, there is a specific source from which that light emanates. Just as the light that strikes the page you are reading has a source—a light bulb, for example—so it is with the light that will illuminate the new heavens and the new earth. That glorious emanation of light proceeds from an identifiable point of origin, from something—rather, Someone—you will be able to recognize!

Compare this to the point John made in the opening statement of his gospel: *"No one has ever seen God; the only Son, who is in the bosom of the Father, he has made him known"* (John 1:18 RSV). I hope it is clear that one of the primary purposes of Jesus' coming into the world was to reveal to us who His Father is. You see, the only way anyone can ever know anything for certain about God's personality or character is through Jesus, His Son. If you were to read only the Old Testament revelation about God, you might come away with mixed signals about who God is. However, one has only to look at the person of Jesus Christ, as revealed in the pages of the New Testament, to realize that all of the characteristics of God harmonize in a most appealing way.

Why is it that Jesus alone has the ability to let us know exactly who God is? Because He was in the beginning with God. He was face-to-face with God. He was God. Who else knows the thoughts and intentions of the heart of God like God? Now, God can be seen clearly in the floodlight of our Savior's luminosity. By simply looking to Jesus, men are at last able to see the Father clearly (John 14:9), discovering that He is a God of burning compassion as well as the God of blazing, uncompromising holiness; a God of beauty and tenderness as well as the Commander in Chief who never makes concessions; a God of blessing who brings nothing but *"healing in His wings"* (Malachi 4:2) as well as the God who creates calamity according to His good purpose (Isaiah 45:7); a God of joy, peace, and love as truly as the One who strikes terror into the hearts of sinful men.

In John's gospel, Jesus is portrayed as *"the light of the world"* (John 8:12), *"the true Light"* (John 1:9) by which all other lights are to be compared. In the book of Revelation, however, we are given quite a different perspective: there we see it is the glory of God the Father that supplies light to the city, but it is the Son who brings definition to that light. At last, we are permitted to see the unapproachable God—not just for a season, but eternally—through the person of our lovely Lord.

The Approachable God

Nevertheless, how could John have described Jesus as a transportable lamp? Is the glory of God Almighty really to be manifested through a movable light? Pardon me if I put this too bluntly, but this is a perfect example of the irony of the Gospel.

This Lamp, John declared, is portable, moveable, or, in simplest terms, touchable! John must have been overwhelmed when he realized that this One who had made His presence known to him on the island of Patmos in such fearsome majesty (remember how John reported in Revelation 1:17 that he fell at Jesus' feet as though dead?) was still accessible and approachable!

Oh, beloved of God, has it really dawned upon your heart of hearts that you, too, on that fine day, will be able to throw your arms around Him? Do you realize that you, too, will be able to look deep into His eyes, just as the disciples of old did?

But, here is the culmination: because Jesus has chosen thus to tabernacle Himself forevermore in human flesh (compare Luke 24:39 with 1 Corinthians 15:21), He will, as well, forevermore remain a faithful and obedient Son:

> [27] *For "[God the Father] has put all things under [Jesus'] feet." But when He says "all things are put under Him," it is evident that He who put all things under Him is excepted.*
> [28] *Now when all things are made subject to Him, then the Son Himself will also be subject to Him who put all things under Him, that God may be all in all.*
>
> (1 Corinthians 15:27–28)

Please take the time to meditate upon this incredible passage. As you are well aware, before our Lord came to Earth as *"the second Man"* (1 Corinthians 15:47), He was *"in the form of God"* (Philippians 2:6), very God of very God. Indeed, He was the Word, the Light, and the Life all rolled into one. But, when He *"emptied himself, taking the form of a servant, being born in the likeness of men"* (Philippians 2:7 RSV), He became a man to remain a man forever. Necessarily, as the Second Adam, and the example to all of His brothers and sisters through the new birth, He will forevermore be subject to God, even as the first Adam ought to have been.

What humility! To choose to step down from His regal position as the One who created the light, as well as the eyes to see it, to become the Vessel who now bears the light so that all may see. Where else has the world ever known such a thing? Who else but Jesus is at once both King of Kings and the willing servant of both God and man?

It is only with the heart that one can see rightly;
what is essential is invisible to the eye.

—Saint-Exupery
The Little Prince

Chapter 13

The Same Yesterday, Today, and Forever

According to the apostle John, the *"New Jerusalem"* (Revelation 21:2)—actually a scintillating synonym for the church, the bride of Christ—shines with the very glory of God. *"Its radiance like a most rare jewel, like a jasper, clear as crystal"* (v. 11 RSV), or, as he said further on in his description, *"transparent as glass"* (v. 21 RSV).

Just how transparent are you, dear friend? Could our Lord say of you, as He did of Nathanael (John 1:47), that you are without guile or deceit? Do you ever pretend to be something you're not? Are you ever guilty of duplicity or disguising your true intentions or feelings?

Isn't it wonderful that, when it comes to Jesus, what you see is what you get? Have you ever thought about the fact that there is no hypocrisy with Jesus, no two-facedness, no deceit? Our Savior is as transparent as glass. When the first disciples looked at Him as He walked and talked among them, they could see nothing but the glory of God, because nothing of the world, the flesh, or the Devil got in the way. Because Jesus is as completely transparent now as He was then, He is able to make everything we need to know about God as *"clear as crystal."*

Christ's Light Shines Through

So also will it be in heaven concerning the church, the bride of Christ. The glory of God will radiate in and through us, the New Jerusalem, the Bible says, because we will be as *"transparent as glass."* That's a promise! May God hasten that day.

In the meantime, many of us feel like we're fully exposed in this world, sitting in glass houses full of tarnished mirrors and smudged windows. Most of us are probably convinced that when our peers look at us, all they can see is our smeared, dirty faces. Yet, wonder of wonders, in spite of how we may feel about the matter, the light of Christ's glory keeps shining through us!

We have learned that when physical light passes through a dense medium, it has the amazing capability of resuming its original speed instantaneously. It is just as if there had been nothing there to slow it down in the first place. So it is with our Lord. Sometimes in our walk and in our talk, a lot of "me, myself, and I" can get in the way, but Jesus has a way of getting through in spite of us. It doesn't take much, either—mostly just our willing hearts.

Have you ever looked through a telescope? If you have, you might have a better idea of what I'm talking about. If you had carefully inspected the mirror of a large telescope that is constantly exposed to the elements, you might have wondered how an image could be seen through the eyepiece of the telescope at all. An unprotected mirror that is open to the weather might have all kinds of dust, dirt, and other contaminants on it—you would be surprised just how dirty a major observatory's mirror can get before the time and trouble is taken to clean it. However, the light gathered by the telescope's mirror seems little affected by the grime. By the time the optics focus the collected light rays into the narrow beam that comes through the eyepiece, the image that it carries can still be clearly seen, even if it came from an object light years away.

Although on the surface—because of all the filth that constantly surrounds us—we may feel rather gritty at times, the light of Christ's glory keeps on shining through. It's humbling to realize, I know, but the reason for it seldom has anything to do with us. Even when we think of ourselves as being at our best, it is only because His focus is upon us that the world is able to see His image in us.

The Constancy of Christ

Does this sound strange? Can the Holy God who calls us out of the world to live godly lives uphold imperfection? Yes, He can, and He does—all the time! (Believe it or not, there are even greater anomalies than this in the kingdom of God.) What we fail to recognize in our self-centeredness is that none of this depends on us, fortunately. Christ remains the same as He operates through us, just as the speed of light returns to its original rate after having passed through a dense medium (and some of us can be quite dense), where its speed resumes its consistency, independent of the medium.

Call this "the other side of grace," if you will, but let us be honest about who we are. Who of us is perfect or without guilt? How many of us have ever experienced even one day or week without blowing it? Or, to phrase it in another way, which one of us is right now what we one day will become?

Please understand that we're not talking here about "cheap grace" or "sloppy agape." We're not talking about willfully living in sin or maintaining the lifestyle of a sinner while God looks the other way. What we're talking about is simply reality. As the apostle Paul expressed it,

> [12] *Not that I have already attained, or am already perfected; but I press on, that I may lay hold of that for which Christ Jesus has also laid hold of me.*
>
> (Philippians 3:12)

Do you see this as applicable to you? Take this idea personally, by telling yourself this:

> Jesus Christ has *"laid hold of me."* Jesus continues to love me, even when my love for Him may waver; He continues to intercede on my behalf, even when I fail to do so on the behalf of others; He continues to serve me in joy and humility, even when I serve Him halfheartedly or not at all. He never withholds His hand of blessing from me; He never removes His Spirit from me. He does not vacillate in His attitude toward me. He just keeps right on wooing, convicting, and comforting—because He is

completely unaffected by my many imper-
fections and inconsistencies. Hallelujah,
what a Savior!

Moreover, even though His church has
gotten a lot of bad press lately, our Lord has
assured us that nothing will ever bury it[1]—not
the true church, His body, His bride. Indeed,
our Lord Himself made it clear that the tares
of this world must be allowed to grow up with
the genuine wheat. (See Matthew 13:24–30.)
He has also warned the wheat and the tares
alike that the chaff will one day be consumed
"with unquenchable fire" (Matthew 3:12).

But as the true church, the bride of Christ,
waits expectantly for her Bridegroom, He has
made another promise: He will cause you to be
without any spots or even a single blemish
when He comes back to take you unto Himself.
(See Ephesians 5:27 and Philippians 1:6.) As a
matter of fact, even though you may be totally
unaware of it, He is in the process of trans-
forming you even as you read the words on this
page. What you are experiencing in your life—
the heartaches, trials, blessings, and triumphs
—are all part of the transformation process.

---

[1] See Matthew 16:18. *"The gateways of death's
grave shall not gain mastery over it"* is a faithful
rendering of the original Greek.

So, take great satisfaction in the fact that although He never changes, He is ever in the process of changing you from one degree of glory to another (2 Corinthians 3:18).

Not only does He keep right on blessing His bride, ready to forgive and eager to cleanse, He keeps on loving this sin-sick, dying world of ours. He continues to pray, *"Father, forgive them, for they do not know what they do"* (Luke 23:34), and will continue to do so until the day when men's hearts have grown so dark and cold that they are beyond repentance. Jesus is still *"the light of the world"* (John 8:12), and the world's darkness has neither overcome it nor diminished it.

> [45] *He makes His sun rise on the evil and on the good, and sends rain on the just and on the unjust.*   (Matthew 5:45)

Our Lord still displays His grace to drug dealers and prostitutes, to hoods and drive-by shooters. Although He abhors their heinous sins, He still loves the corrupt politician and the serial killer, the abortionist and the child molester. This is inconceivable, isn't it? That is why it's called grace! Grace is something undeserved. God's grace is extravagant, and the reason it is extravagant is because of its focal point: through Christ Jesus, that focus is, always has been, and always will be the cross and Christ's shed blood.

The Mysterious Nature of the God-Man

I want to compare one more facet of physical light, which we have already discussed, to Jesus. The characteristic of how light is propagated is the very essence of what makes physical light so unique and what reveals the singularity of *"the light of the world."*

Unlike any other physical phenomenon, light seems to exhibit certain well-defined properties when viewed one way; yet, when looked at in another way, it exhibits properties that are wholly incompatible with the first set. Logically speaking, light doesn't make sense.

Nevertheless, scientists and theoreticians the world over seem content enough with the fact that light remains a mystery. Of course, the reason they are content is obvious: they have no other choice. To date, the properties of light are inexplicable and enigmatic. Yet, although no one can explain light, light keeps right on shining—making it possible for scientists to keep on doing their experiments and theoreticians to keep on writing down their endless theories.

With this in mind, I find it particularly fascinating that, without apology, the Bible plainly states Jesus Christ encompasses both the dynamics of deity and the humility of humanity at the same time. As we have seen, the apostle Paul has summed up that fact quite succinctly in one concise phrase: *"For in Him dwells all the fullness of the Godhead bodily"* (Colossians 2:9).

Talk about the inexplicable! How can all the glory of the Godhead reside in a tabernacle of human flesh? How can Jesus simultaneously be both God and man? How can it be that God the Son, the second person of the Trinity, will remain subject to His Father for all of time and eternity? This enigmatic One, whom we are not only privileged to behold, but to embrace as our own Lord and Savior, is nothing less than the One the Bible calls *"the light of the world."*

Yet the vast majority of intellectuals, who have no problem accepting the incongruities of physical light, balk at the biblical assertion that Jesus is both God and man. There is something inconsistent here, all right, but I think it has to do with the double standards of the scholastic community rather than any supposed inconsistencies in the One who is the Mystery of the Ages.

Nevertheless, our precious Lord keeps on extending His grace, forgiving those who speak His name only in vain. He continues to sustain the universe *"by the word of His power"* (Hebrews 1:3), even though His creation continues to ignore Him. He still causes the rain to fall upon the just and the unjust and the sun to shine upon the evil and the good (Matthew 5:45). How unfathomable are the riches of His grace (Ephesians 3:8), how profound is His mercy, and how penetrating is His humility!

The Incomprehensible Light of the World

"The light of the world" is knowable and yet unsearchable. To this very day, no one has been able to comprehend Him. Certainly it is Jesus who is and ever will be "a riddle wrapped in a mystery inside an enigma!"[2] Our most celebrated thinkers have yet to fathom Him. Our most preeminent theologians are still baffled by Him. Without Him nothing can exist that does exist (John 1:3), but no one who exists is able to fully grasp all that He is. Jesus, *"the light of the world,"* truly defies definition!

Yet, just as the velocity of light is the only known constant in the physical universe,

---

[2] Attributed to Winston Churchill

The Same Yesterday, Today, and Forever

"Jesus Christ is the same yesterday, today, and forever" (Hebrews 13:8). In this world of ever-changing values, where the only thing you can count on is that you can't count on anything, Jesus Christ still stands firm. He is *"the Rock of our salvation"* (Psalm 95:1), the sure ground of our being, our help and our shield (Psalm 33:20), our bulwark against the flood, and a safe haven from life's storms.

> ² *The LORD is my rock and my fortress and my deliverer; My God, my strength, in whom I will trust; My shield and the horn of my salvation, my stronghold.* (Psalm 18:2)

All around us earthquakes and cataclysms threaten body and soul. Indeed, the Bible warns us that the time is soon coming when men will faint with foreboding and fear of what is coming upon the world, for the very powers of the heavens will be shaken. Surely, that day is right around the corner! We have discovered we can't depend upon anything on Earth—that's for certain. Governments are corrupt; societies are in shambles; educational institutions are in disrepair; religious traditions are in turmoil. Few say what they mean or mean·what they say. Many of our political leaders are morally bankrupt, and, sadly, many of our spiritual leaders are no less suspect.

But, through all of this, Jesus Christ hasn't changed. Oh, what a comfort and solace to the struggling heart and weary mind! If He were to suddenly appear in your living room or study, or wherever you may be reading this, you can be sure of this one thing: He would be exactly the same as when He was last seen on Earth.

Admittedly, this might be a problem for some, simply because Jesus is the same pure, uncompromised Lord and King that He was when He first walked among men. In fact, His very presence might elicit from some lips only a hushed, *"Depart from me, for I am a sinful man, O Lord"* (Luke 5:8).

However, who would want it otherwise? Wouldn't you rather stand condemned in your sins than discover Jesus was a sham? Wouldn't you rather shudder under His holy gaze than look into eyes that revealed only deep-seated pride and hypocrisy? Aren't you relieved when you realize that there actually is Someone who is not only holy, but utterly transparent?

Not only is Jesus undefiled and blameless, but He is absolutely and unequivocally dependable! You can count on His purity when you look in His eyes. You will never wonder if lust lies hidden deep within His heart. You can count on Him when the world comes crashing down around you. *"He Himself has said, 'I will never leave you nor forsake you'"* (Hebrews 13:5). You can depend upon His Word. When He says He will save you from your sins, you can bet your life on it! Even when death comes knocking on your door, you can depend upon Jesus answering the strains of "Rock of Ages, Cleft for me, Let me hide myself in Thee," as He sweeps you up in His arms and transports you into realms of glory.

How different it is with so many who claim to follow Him in this day and age. We who are so full of ourselves, who have the blatancy to exalt and lift up ourselves before Him, nonetheless fail Him and others so predictably. Yet, He still meets our every need with meekness and grace, but not because He is at our beck and call—as some in the kingdom have had the audacity even to teach. Far from it! Our Savior does so because He is incredibly long-suffering and kind in His humility.

What a Sure Foundation!

Fascinatingly, in a world where textbooks in physics become outdated every year and where every child who has ever seen *Jurassic Park* is convinced that chaos is cool, light still does what it does in exactly the ways it has always done from the beginning of time. Even more captivating is that in spite of all the liberals and modernists and reconstructionists and so-called "Jesus Seminars," Jesus hasn't changed one bit to accommodate anyone's opinion of Him! *"Jesus Christ is the same yesterday, today, and forever"* (Hebrews 13:8).

You theologians, take note. Did you know that Jesus Christ is greater than the greatest thought you have ever had about Him? Are you aware, dear friend, that your theology cannot contain Him any more than your eloquence can describe Him and that your uncertainty hasn't deterred Him any more than your worry can shake Him? Still, incredibly, your faith and trust in Him always, always moves Him!

And behold, I am coming quickly,
and My reward is with Me,
to give to every one according to his work.
I am the Alpha and the Omega,
the Beginning and the End,
the First and the Last.

—Jesus Christ
Revelation 22:12–13

Chapter 14

In Awe of the Servant King

In his letter to the Ephesians, the apostle Paul wrote: *"I pray also that the eyes of your heart may be enlightened"* (Ephesians 1:18 NIV). This is my prayer as well, both for myself and for you, my readers. If we are to gain anything of a godly perspective as we approach the written Word, we must lay aside our prejudices and preconceived ideas; we must ask the Holy Spirit to impart to us *"the mind of Christ"* (1 Corinthians 2:16)—most especially when it comes to matters relating to the Christ.

Jesus, the Messiah, the *monogenes* (the "only begotten") of God, and our Savior, actually walked among men. His coming into the world the first time was the most significant event in the history of the universe. Moreover, His next appearing will eclipse His first.

What kind of a man was He? What kind of a man is He? Why does Jesus, and Jesus alone, have a rightful claim to my life as my very Lord and Master? Why and how did He accomplish the things He did on Earth? And how will He go about establishing His kingdom when He comes again?

If we are less than astonished by our Lord and His sacrifice, we have probably missed much of the Gospel. And, if we are content to be less than interested about such matters or apathetic about the nature of the One whom we serve, it is only because we have probably taken our Lord for granted. It is my fondest hope, of course, that, if nothing else, my study will stimulate us to think much about Jesus. But in so saying, I acknowledge, along with the apostle Paul, that true enlightenment about spiritual things can only come by a revelation of God to our hearts.

It is my fervent prayer, therefore, that all of us may, with the eyes of our hearts, catch a glimpse of the Lamb of God, the Light of the World, the heavenly Lamp, our Bridegroom. Once we have caught sight of who He really is, we are virtually guaranteed a lifetime—indeed, an eternity—of blessed wonder.

I also pray that if I have written anything in the flesh or without understanding, it would never be allowed to take root in either your heart or mine. However, if what has been written here is of God, may it serve as an impetus for us all to know Him even more; for to know Jesus, I am persuaded, is to love Him.

Let it also be known that where I am personally concerned, it is Jesus alone who has the right to my allegiance; it is He alone who has found the key to my heart!

Admittedly, in this all-too-brief look that God has granted me to have of His Anointed, Jesus' deity overwhelms me. Equally true is that Jesus' humanity inspires me. However, I gratefully confess with a song of praise upon my lips, it is Jesus' humility that makes me want to fall before Him, kiss His feet, and then rise again, only to follow Him all the rest of my days!

May it be the same with you, dear reader.

About the Author

After witnessing a tragic accident at nineteen years of age, Verne Nesbitt found himself on his knees pleading with God to save him through the shed blood of Christ. From that moment on, he knew deep within that he would serve the Lord for the rest of his life.

In the course of his ministry, Verne acquired degrees in both theology and philosophy, which equipped him to teach philosophy and apologetics as well as biblical studies at Rockmont College (now Colorado Christian University) in Denver and at Westmont College on the West Coast. Concurrently, he served as senior pastor for several churches in California and Arizona.

For the past dozen years, Verne has served as a resource speaker for Youth with a Mission (YWAM) at the University of the Nations in Hawaii and at numerous mission bases around the world. He has traveled extensively throughout Europe, Africa, Latin America, and the Pacific Rim nations, teaching and ministering to those both within and without the body of Christ.

During the course of his journeys, he has had the privilege of ministering to government officials of the Communist Party of the People's Republic of China. As a consequence of a preaching tour in Romania, he became a founding board member of Family-to-Family Romanian Outreach Ministries.

Happily married for over 38 years, Verne and his wife Diane have four children who, to date, have presented them with nine grandchildren. When they are not ministering elsewhere, they reside in Phoenix, Arizona.